LIMPING HEAVENWARD

Living by Faith in Comprehensive and Chronic Suffering

KARRIE HAHN

P&R PUBLISHING

P.O. BOX 817 • PHILLIPSBURG • NEW JERSEY 08865-0817

Relevant Scripture quotations from the New Testament use the ESV's alternate, footnoted translation of *adelphoi* ("brothers and sisters").

Italics within Scripture quotations indicate emphasis added.

Cover design by Francisco Adolfo Hernández Aceves

Printed in the United States of America

Library of Congress Cataloging-in-Publication Data

Names: Hahn, Karrie author
Title: Limping heavenward : living by faith in comprehensive and chronic
  suffering / Karrie Hahn.
Description: Phillipsburg, New Jersey : P&R Publishing Company, [2025] |
  Summary: "When prolonged, all-encompassing suffering decimates life,
  sufferers face painful questions about God-and unhelpful responses from
  others. Avoiding "miserable comfort," Hahn turns to Scripture for truths
  that build hope and endurance"-- Provided by publisher.
Identifiers: LCCN 2025018231 | ISBN 9798887791647 paperback | ISBN
  9798887791654 epub
Subjects: LCSH: Suffering--Religious aspects--Christianity |
  Suffering--Biblical teaching | Consolation
Classification: LCC BV4909 .H34 2025 | DDC 248.8/6--dc23/
  eng/20250625
LC record available at https://lccn.loc.gov/2025018231

Limping is often the right word to describe the journey heavenward for those entangled in the world of chronic pain and illness. This book takes no shortcuts and refuses to skirt around the jagged rocks on the path. It's honest, and its honesty and faithfulness are a welcome light in the darkness.

    —**Nate Brooks**, Author, *Disrupted Journey*

Limping Heavenward is a deeply compassionate and theologically rich guide that offers comfort, understanding, and practical help to those who are enduring long-term suffering. Karrie skillfully intertwines personal experiences with the timeless truths of Scripture, offering readers empathy and encouragement. This book is not only a comfort to sufferers but also an invaluable resource for those who seek to support them with grace and understanding.

    —**Shannon Kay McCoy**, Counselor, Speaker, Author

Karrie Hahn's debut work is an insightful and intimate look into chronic and comprehensive suffering. From Job to Jeremiah, Hahn weaves her harrowing story of suffering with the rich treasures of Scripture, keeping her steady and determined gaze on Jesus Christ. I have every confidence that her work will help countless sufferers feel seen and known.

    —**Jonathan D. Holmes**, Executive Director, Fieldstone Counseling

If you experience ongoing suffering and have struggled to find relatable help, this book is for you. Karrie Hahn has much hard-earned wisdom to share. Filled with nuanced discussion and thoughtful insights drawn from Scripture, *Limping Heavenward* will encourage a fuller, more hopeful perspective as you live with comprehensive suffering.

    —**Esther Smith**, Author, *A Still and Quiet Mind*

Limping Heavenward is a biblically and theologically grounded and deeply personal book written by a Christian who has walked through affliction and still clings to her Savior, who so faithfully holds her close. Karrie Hahn does not offer detached counsel from outside the storm but writes from within it, sharing how the Lord has faithfully sustained her through years of chronic suffering. Her words echo a Scottish theologian's poignant observation that the Christian life is "falling down and getting up, all the way to heaven." This is a book for fellow pilgrims, for those who need encouragement to keep going when everything hurts and hope seems remote. I'm grateful for this honest and faithful testimony to the sustaining grace of God.

—**Chris Larson**, President & CEO, Ligonier Ministries

Limping Heavenward is a tender and wise companion for those who walk long, lonely roads of suffering. With honesty and theological depth, Karrie Hahn offers dignity to those who bear the soul-crushing weight of comprehensive and chronic affliction. Her words gently reorient weary hearts to the steadfast presence of Christ. This book is a lifeline for those who feel forgotten—and for the church that is called to love them.

—**Darby Strickland**, Faculty, Christian Counseling & Educational Foundation; Author, *When It's Trauma*

To those who feel unseen, unheard, afraid, and
alone in their suffering, this book is for you.

"Let him who walks in darkness and has no light
trust in the name of the Lord and rely on his God."
Isaiah 50:10

"And after you have suffered a little while,
the God of all grace, who has called you
to his eternal glory in Christ,
will himself restore, confirm,
strengthen, and establish you.
To him be the dominion forever and ever.
Amen."
1 Peter 5:10–11

CONTENTS

Introduction   7

Part 1: Relational Struggles in Suffering

   1. Orienting Ourselves   15

   2. Miserable Comforters   33

   3. The Ancient Serpent   55

   4. The God Who Is   71

Part 2: Comprehensive and Chronic Suffering

   5. How God Treats His Friends   99

   6. The Wait of Glory   115

Part 3: Living with Suffering

   7. Weeping in Hurt   133

   8. Rejoicing in Hope   151

   Conclusion   173

   Appendix: How to Help Those Who Face Comprehensive and Chronic Suffering   175

   Notes   191

INTRODUCTION

Why another book on suffering? It's a fair question to ask. Books on the topic abound, and many of them are helpful. But suffering is like the human face: Though we all have eyes, a nose, and a mouth, there's endless variety to how each part is arranged, making us unique and setting us apart from others. Suffering is similar, in that common features may be present in our stories, but there's also diversity in the shape of that suffering in each of our lives. Because we all experience different suffering and experience suffering differently—and because suffering in a fallen world is an undeniable, ever-present reality—it is good for us to have as many biblically faithful and practically helpful resources as possible.

A more personal answer to the question is that I've read many books on suffering, but most of them didn't address the specific questions or issues I was struggling with. That's not because they were bad books, but rather because every book is limited in what it can cover and who it can reach. I kept finding that three of the major aspects of my own suffering weren't being addressed in detail, leaving my biggest questions and challenges also unaddressed.

The first missing aspect relates to the *totality* of the suffering. That is, many books approach suffering from the perspective of the "one big thing" going wrong in life, while the rest of life remains relatively stable. For example, they might say, "Perhaps you're dealing with financial difficulties. Or maybe you're experiencing problems with your health. Or you might have lost relationships that were very precious to you." When reading these books, I remember thinking, "But *everything* the author listed is happening to me. Where's the book that addresses what to do when *all* the pillars holding up your life crash down around you rather than just one or two?"

The second missing aspect has to do with the *longevity* of such suffering. Many books approach suffering in the context of a season of one's life that will come and go. While they may acknowledge that the suffering may be lifelong, they don't aim to help people in such circumstances live out the implications of this hard truth or address the difficult questions that arise from ongoing suffering. To put it another way, how do we move forward in faith when crisis suffering settles into chronic suffering?

The third missing aspect relates to how these two types of suffering together—which I refer to as *comprehensive and chronic suffering*—can deeply disrupt a person's relationship with God and relationships with others. Of course, all books on suffering are bound to discuss these relational aspects to some extent. But I hope to address questions and struggles in these areas that may be less emphasized or not covered in other books.

That said, this book aims to accomplish the following purposes: (1) to address the particular struggles that can arise from the kind of suffering that results in losses within *many different areas* of a person's life—physical health, finances, friendships, job and career, church, family, and home and belongings; (2) to address the particular struggles that arise from suffering that is *more than just a season* and will likely have to be endured throughout the rest of one's life; (3) to speak to those who find themselves grappling with deep, hard, and painful questions about who God is and his posture toward them in light of their comprehensive and chronic suffering; (4) to identify and address how those seeking to be "helpers" can actually cause more suffering and pain; and (5) to wrestle to connect comprehensive and chronic suffering to the God of the Bible in ways that restore faith, confidence, peace, endurance, and hope.

This book is especially targeted to those who

- feel stuck in or overwhelmed by their comprehensive and chronic suffering;
- struggle to believe that God is good and that his Word is true in light of their circumstances; and
- feel the absence of God and/or the absence of his people in their time of greatest need.

To all who resonate with these challenges, I hope that this book provides at least one transformative truth to sustain you in the faith. It is written for those enduring particularly deep, difficult, and long-term suffering, loss, and affliction. It is for those whose circumstances have almost crushed their souls and extinguished their faith. It is for those asking anguished questions in the heat of the battle rather than the comfort of the classroom. It is for those who wonder if God has forgotten to be gracious to them and who are lost in a fog of confusion despite their biblical and theological knowledge.

At the same time, this book can also be valuable for believers who aren't presently enduring comprehensive and chronic suffering. Though we don't all experience the same degree of suffering, we all experience it to some extent, and the questions and struggles that arise from suffering often share the same spiritual DNA. God's Word speaks to all sufferers, providing the framework through which we can understand and interpret the trials and heartaches we face in this life. Moreover, we are part of the body of Christ, and as such, Christian love compels us to care for fellow members in the wisest and most informed ways possible. Toward that end, I hope that this book serves as a guide for what the experience of comprehensive and chronic sufferers entails, as well as how we can better love such sufferers in the church.

Here's the path we'll take. Part 1 centers on how comprehensive and chronic suffering influences and is influenced by our relationships. The four relationships we'll explore are our relationships to ourselves (chapter 1), to other people (chapter 2), to Satan and his minions (chapter 3), and to God (chapter 4). Chapter 4 is particularly significant, as struggles here profoundly shape all the other struggles we face. In part 2, we'll look at some of the unique challenges and questions that arise from comprehensive suffering (chapter 5) and from chronic suffering (chapter 6), turning to Scripture to address some of our unanswered questions and to provide encouragement and hope. In part 3, which builds on all the truths we encountered in parts 1 and 2, we turn to what daily life looks like in comprehensive and chronic suffering, examining what a lifestyle of continual lamenting (chapter 7) and rejoicing (chapter 8) looks like.

Along the way, we'll address questions like these: Is God cruel? Does he play favorites among his children? Does he hate me? Am I doing something wrong? Does he care? Is he really compassionate? Does he hear my prayers? Why do some believers experience more suffering than others? Why has God felt so absent from me, and even hostile toward me, in my deepest anguish? Why does God seem to be wasting my life? How can I endure when the suffering has impacted so many parts of what makes life feel "alive" and my circumstances are unlikely to change? Why are other believers leaving me to suffer alone or simply accusing me of sin?

No one book can say everything that needs to be said, and life is not as simple as reading a book and having everything instantly click into place. We are all on a journey of faith, walking with the Lord through difficult places, and no two journeys will look quite the same. But my prayer is that those who are beneath life's crushing load might find encouragement to keep going in the race of faith in the pages that follow. And that is precisely why the book is titled *Limping Heavenward*.

In the race of faith, it doesn't matter how quickly we can run. It just matters that we keep moving in the right direction, toward the Lord, and that we don't give up. Limping isn't less noble or less difficult than running; in fact, sometimes the opposite is true. Our limp is real, but so is the destination of heaven. Our groaning is real, but so is the glory that will one day be revealed to those who, by God's grace, endure to the end.

Relational Struggles in Suffering

1

ORIENTING OURSELVES

It all started on a weekend road trip to Austin, Texas, in June 2012. That weekend split my life in two: There was my life *before* that weekend, and what became my life *after* that weekend.

It came suddenly and out of nowhere. What started as a slight sore throat became the worst sore throat I'd ever experienced in my life. The next day, I grew weaker and weaker as all the energy drained from my body. I was alone at the house where I was staying and had to army crawl to the bathroom because I no longer had the energy to stand or walk. I was taken to an emergency room in Austin, where they said they couldn't find anything wrong with me. I was physically carried out of the ER because I couldn't walk, seriously ill but with no answers.

After a sleepless night, the next morning I was put in the passenger seat of the car in my pajamas, driven back to Dallas, and taken straight to an ER there, where my parents met me. I was admitted to the hospital while they ran a number of tests on me. At one point during the hospitalization, I began to lose the ability to communicate. In my head, I knew the words that I wanted to say, but I couldn't get them to come out of my mouth. My body and brain seemed to be completely out of my control. Then the diagnosis came back: mononucleosis. I had heard of mono, of course. You get really tired for a few weeks and miss school or work, then you get better, right? But this felt like something altogether different.

After two restless days in the hospital, I signed out against medical advice. The constant interruptions and beeping machines throughout the night just made my exhaustion worse. The doctors said that I would get better in a few weeks or months. But I didn't. The earthquake that was set in motion that day came after almost everything in my life. Over the coming weeks and months, it felt like I was standing there frozen, watching almost everything I loved wobble precariously before crashing to the ground in a million tiny pieces, one after another.

Comprehensive Suffering

I use the term *comprehensive suffering* to describe what happens when so many different pillars of a person's world crash down simultaneously that life becomes overwhelming, terrifying, and unstable. It is too much, too fast, and often coincides with too little support from others. Any semblance of normalcy or safety is shattered. When we think about the different categories of life that can be touched by suffering, most fall into the following list: our physical health and bodies, our finances, our church life and ministry, our friendships, our careers, our families, and our homes and belongings.

When we consider examples of comprehensive suffering in Scripture, Job immediately comes to mind. Within a very brief time span, his children were killed, his relationship with his wife became strained, his closest friends deeply wounded him, his wealth disappeared, his belongings were destroyed, and he was afflicted with illness. Worst of all, Job's relationship with God became a disorienting source of terror as he struggled to understand what was happening and why.

After that day in 2012, comprehensive suffering intruded into my life as well. First, my physical health came crashing to the ground. Then, five months into my illness, a dating relationship that had been heading toward marriage—the whole reason I'd been spending the summer in Texas even though I lived in California—ended with a surprise breakup instead, leaving me emotionally shattered. After trying to return to my job and life in California that fall, I relapsed (I had never actually healed in the first place), and my dad had to fly out to bring me back to Texas again to stay with him and my mom so that they could take care of me.

It was incredibly stressful to be sick as a single person and living somewhere else. I still had to deal with my condo, all my bills, and everything else from a different state with no one to help me. I had to try to get my California disability benefits long-distance, which was a monumentally stressful experience, only to receive a fraction of my normal salary. During that winter back in Texas, relationships with some of my work colleagues in California deteriorated, resulting in deeply painful relational breakdowns and accusations.

By the next spring, I had to step down from my full-time job due to my health limitations and relational concerns. This was a loss on multiple levels. I had to leave a ministry position that allowed me to use my gifts to serve others, I lost my sole source of income, and I lost a job that had provided me with a community that had been a source of life, care, and blessing to me as a single woman. It was so much more than leaving a job. It was leaving my entire community, my happy place, my "home."

Still emotionally reeling from all these losses and physically unwell, I pushed myself to find another job to pay my bills. I accepted a seemingly promising job opportunity that ended up being the worst job I've ever had. In the year that followed, I continued to become more and more physically, emotionally, and spiritually drained by the dysfunctional leadership and unhealthy culture that pervaded the organization. I spent many of my lunch breaks crying in a bathroom stall, asking the Lord to rescue me. I was desperate to leave, but I couldn't quit without another job.

I suppose the Lord answered my prayer—but not in a way that made life any easier. That job abruptly ended after a year, when I was called into the office and informed that my position had been eliminated and that I no longer had a job, effective immediately. I was then informed that I would receive no unemployment benefits and sent home.

Now unemployed and with no source of income, I undertook the massive project of having to sell or give away most of my belongings, leave my home of ten years in California, and move halfway across the country to live in a tiny room in my parents' house at the age of thirty-five. As I prepared to leave California, a friend let me use her house for a garage sale. I'll never forget what it felt like to see most of my belongings spread out over a concrete slab, selling for pennies on the dollar, while everything that didn't sell was loaded into trash bags to donate. All the evidence of the "normal" life I'd enjoyed was vanishing before my eyes, and my treasured possessions became trash to dispose of. No area of my life was left untouched.

The metaphorical earthquake didn't take one thing, or two things, or three things. It was comprehensive. (And this was just the beginning. Much more was to come.) It felt like I was sitting amid the ruins of a shattered life with nothing but broken pieces, chaos, and confusion all around. The suffering wasn't neatly cordoned off to just one or two areas of my life. Rather, it was far-reaching in how many areas of my life it ravaged.

This earthquake occurred over a period of about two years. So, while it was comprehensive, it was not yet chronic. It was still an acute situation, a supposed "season" that I and everyone else expected would be resolved in the coming months after I moved back to Texas. But my health did not improve after the move; it actually got worse. I became partially homebound as my body shut down on me.

In retrospect, the sheer breadth and depth of so many losses so close together was more than my body or soul could take, and I didn't have time and space to process the losses, nor anyone to process them with. Even though I was sick, I had to keep working to pay my bills and retain medical insurance since I didn't have a spouse to support me, producing a crushing amount of emotional stress over my finances and worsening my physical condition.

I also felt pressure to keep pushing spiritually. It seemed as though many of the people around me did not want to hear me cry or were not willing to lament my losses with me. To the contrary, the people around me said I needed to be more joyful in my suffering, more content with my life circumstances, more trusting in the Lord. It was clear that to some, I hadn't proven I was "godly" enough in my suffering, and my spiritual maturity was now in question.

After I had lived that way for two years, my body completely shut down in exhaustion. Looking back, I see that I had been pushing myself on sheer adrenaline for far too long. But after returning to Texas to figure out my next steps in a radically disrupted life, my body seemed to sense that rest was possible and decided to shut down on me.

I had fully expected that after losing so much, the Lord would allow me to start over again in Texas, though starting from square one in my mid-thirties felt daunting. I had imagined that within a few months, I'd be physically healthy, get a new job, move into my own apartment, find a church community, rebuild a new network of friends, and maybe even get married while I was still young enough to have children. But none of that happened.

It's interesting to note that when we look at Job's story in Scripture, right on the heels of comprehensive loss, Job responded with worship. It was still an acute situation for him. The pain was raw, but it wasn't yet ongoing. But as days and weeks turned into months, we see Job being worn down as his faith started to manifest itself differently than in the early days when he declared, "The Lord gave, and the Lord has taken away; blessed be the name of the Lord" (Job 1:21).

Chronic Suffering

In the years that followed, my acute suffering morphed into chronic suffering, and I did not experience the renewal and restoration that I and others had hoped and prayed for. Instead, my life seemed to hit a dead end, and I felt completely trapped within the four walls of my room in my parents' house. That's when the chronic aspect of the suffering entered my experience: I felt trapped in a hallway.

No matter how many jobs I applied for, no viable opportunities came. Because I had always had a heart for ministry, I had no experience in a secular career path that would provide adequate financial compensation. The options were pathetically few. On the rare occasions that I did get an offer, it was either too low-paying to make ends meet or impossible to do with my health limitations, so I continued to drain my savings. I tried to get involved at a new church, but relationships like the ones I'd had in California just didn't form. I didn't make many new friends, and I was painfully lonely. Having to live with my parents due to my financial situation meant living in a suburban area that was predominantly families with young children, and very few people seemed able to connect with a single woman with no children. I felt like an alien, a cultural oddity. And the entire time, I was going from doctor to doctor in search of a diagnosis for the crushing exhaustion and painful neurological symptoms that were destroying my life yet refusing to reveal their identity despite all the medical tests that were being run.

As the years went by, my hope of getting married and having children faded. After all, who would want to marry me—a chronically ill woman who wouldn't be able to have kids or live a normal life? And even if someone did want to marry me, what would I do if he started having health problems too, since I could barely take care of myself? As physical and financial problems continued to weigh me down like a crushing load, my hope of moving out of my parents' house into my own place ebbed away. As medical treatment after medical treatment failed to cure my mysterious condition, my hope of functioning like a normal adult again died a slow death. And as meaningful friendships and relationships continued to elude me, my hope of ever feeling connected or part of a caring community again withered.

Not having meaningful work to do made my life feel purposeless. Both my physical condition and the lack of work left me isolated and alone in my room most days, reading or staring out my window at a crape myrtle tree, as spring, summer, fall, and winter cycled through over and over. The terror of my financial situation haunted me relentlessly, the stress worsening my physical condition. And another dating relationship that had held out the promise of being the ever-elusive "reason" why the Lord had allowed my life to come crashing down and brought me to Texas ended as miserably as the previous relationship had. The more I tried to make sense of it all and discern God's purpose, the less sense everything seemed to make, and the less I could discern God's purposes at all.

It felt like I was in a hallway lined with doors on both sides. I was desperately pounding on the doors and jiggling locked knobs, but God wasn't opening any of them for me in my attempts to start over again. I continued running up and down the hallway, banging on every door I could find, grabbing every doorknob I could get a hold of. But nothing changed. Eventually, I slumped to the floor in an exhausted heap. What do you do when you try your best to start a new life after your old life is taken away, but you find yourself permanently locked in the hallway? Why was a sovereign and good God keeping me trapped and preventing me from starting over? I felt like the remaining belongings I'd brought back to Texas and put in a small storage unit a few miles away. They lay there in boxes in the dark, collecting dust—unseen, unused, not fulfilling the purposes for which they were created.

We can display incredible resilience and fortitude in crisis. Our bodies and souls gear up for battle. In the beginning, when a situation is fresh and acute, we have strength to fight. Our adrenaline and cortisol are pumping. While acute suffering may be hard, its limited and relatively short duration doesn't tax our resources to their dregs. We have enough strength to endure a season, and the people around us are most comfortable and familiar with supporting us in brief, acute seasons of suffering, especially if others are advocating for us or making our needs known.

But when days turn into months and months turn into years with little change or improvement, and when we're doing it essentially alone, that's a different story altogether. Our human resources of strength, faith, and wisdom don't extend that far or that deep. After all, hallways are meant to take us from one place to another; they're not meant to be places where we live. Yet chronic suffering can feel like taking up residence in a hallway; we are stuck in a purgatory between the life we once had, which is now inaccessible, and a new life we want to start but that keeps eluding us, ever out of our grasp despite our best efforts.

We see this in Job's story as well. As suffering goes on with no resolution, his triumphant declaration of faith at the beginning of the book turns into the long middle section of the book, where we find bewildered and excruciating dialogues of a faith stretched almost to the breaking point. We can often endure a short-lived, major crisis. We can often endure chronic but low-grade suffering. But who can endure a chronic crisis? And, as we see in the book of Job, this type of suffering can often be compounded by unhelpful or unloving responses from the people around us.

But the very worst part of this suffering is what can happen in our relationship with God. Job's greatest distress in all his suffering was how it led to great anguish and confusion about God's character and his posture toward Job. So perhaps the better question is this: Who can endure a chronic crisis apart from the knowledge that a loving and powerful God is not *against* us but *for* us in our affliction (see Ps. 56:9)? What do we do when our lives feel like a story that God just got tired of writing and abandoned midcourse?

External Circumstances Versus Internal Anguish

When we talk about the things that happen to us or to others, we're speaking about external circumstances. This is primarily a communication of the facts: It's the *whats* that have happened to us. For example, we lost a job, we got sick, our spouse or child died, our house burned down, we went through a divorce, or we experienced a rupture in a relationship. But these *whats* are just the tip of the iceberg that lies beneath: how these external circumstances impact our emotions, minds, faith, and relationship to God. This internal anguish is much harder to explain to other people, because no matter what words we use, they feel inadequate to convey the gravity of the situation and the desolation of our soul.

Comprehensive and chronic suffering can result in profound inner anguish as we struggle to orient ourselves both to what we're enduring and to how it's internally affecting us. I felt profound terror and anxiety during the first weeks when the mono was acute. I had no control over my own body and experienced mysterious physical episodes of weakness, faintness, malaise, and not feeling "right" in my own body. It actually felt like I was in the process of dying. When the dating relationship ended, I was emotionally shattered. It happened unexpectedly during my acute illness, and that relationship had been one of my only sources of stability in the present or hope for the future. When that came crashing down, I was more than heartbroken. It almost destroyed me. I remember screaming (literally) to the Lord in prayer, telling him that if he didn't help me, I wouldn't survive. Without his strength, I had no hope of making it through.

As relationships with friends and colleagues also deteriorated, I was filled with grief, sadness, shame, and loneliness. It hurt to lose friendships I had treasured. It made me feel shame to be told that I wasn't godly enough in my suffering. I was confronted by a close friend for not being "cheerful" enough while ill; another time, a friend asked whether I was pretending that my illness was worse than it really was. I remember lying on the hard floor of my kitchen one night, sobbing after attempts at reconciling relationships had fallen flat, so filled with grief and pain that I thought I might actually die of a broken heart. I felt guilty that I apparently hadn't been brave enough or strong enough in my suffering despite my best attempts.

As time went on and things didn't get better, discouragement led to depression, and depression gave way to despair. I kept journaling, trying to figure out what God was trying to "teach" me and racking my brain for how my sin might be causing my suffering. I lost any sense of God's presence, love, or care for me as, spiritually, everything seemed to go dark. Sometimes I felt excruciating emotional pain; other times I felt numbness, since not feeling at all was sometimes better than constantly feeling too much. Eventually, I forgot what it felt like to be happy.

I also felt like a misfit at church and with other Christians, awkwardly trying to participate in conversations that revolved around the "normal" things of life that everyone else had but that were foreign to me. I tried to smile and nod on the outside, but inside the alienation from other believers only worsened my suffering. It felt like I was alone in a rowboat on the ocean in a massive storm, overwhelmed by winds and waves, just trying to survive. But when I went to church or small group, everyone else sounded like they were sailing on a cruise. It did not appear that we were in the same boat at all. After so many attempts to build new friendships fell flat, I began to feel ashamed, wondering if I was no longer fun to be around or worthy of friendship or considered desirable by others. I wondered, perhaps, if others thought I was just not worthy of being known or loved.

The constant financial pressures produced chronic stress, as I felt helpless and alone, unsafe and insecure. Thinking about the future terrified me. Who would care for me when my parents died and I had no spouse, no children, no friends? Who would be there for me if I had an emergency or was hospitalized? How could I endure if the physical pain became worse? And how could I bear to be so alone every day for the rest of my life? I felt abandoned by others in my suffering, and worst of all, I felt abandoned by God. I remember sitting in the pink chair in the corner of my room one day, experiencing a moment that felt like my faith got sucked out of my soul and there was nothing left. I simply didn't have the strength to go on any longer. Something inside me broke.

Theologian R.C. Sproul notes, "Suffering is one of the most significant challenges to any believer's faith. When pain, grief, persecution, or other forms of suffering strike, we find ourselves caught off guard, confused, and full of questions. Suffering can strain faith to the limits."[1] Indeed, suffering can strain faith to the limits, especially when it's both comprehensive and chronic.

Prepared for Suffering?

Comprehensive and chronic suffering often brings us to a new frontier. It forces us out of a comfortable, predictable, settled land into a harsh, uninhabited wilderness. Paul Tripp observes, "Suffering takes us to the borders of our faith. It leads us to think about things we've never thought about before and maybe even question things we thought were settled in our hearts."[2] Because of this, we should not be shocked if comprehensive and chronic suffering impacts our view of the world or brings us to painful places in our relationship with God that we would never have expected.

We often hear the sentiment in modern evangelicalism that if we just arm ourselves with enough biblical truth before the tsunami of suffering hits, then we can triumphantly sail through any affliction with otherworldly joy, peace, strength, and confidence. But that sentiment is often inaccurate, and it sometimes borders on arrogance or presumption. Of course we should store up God's Word in our hearts and learn all that we can about his character and his ways. But ultimately, we can't entirely inoculate ourselves against the profound impact of deep and lengthy affliction, for if Satan aims to destroy our faith (and he does), we would expect it to stretch us right up to the border of our breaking point.

Job was the most righteous man of his day (see Job 1:1), but his godly maturity did not prevent his going to very painful and dark places in comprehensive and chronic suffering. It won't prevent our going there either. But the good news is that God shepherds us into and leads us through the dark places, even when we can't see him or feel him there at all. Many of God's beloved children have found themselves in such places, so if we find ourselves there as well, we are not alone.

Suffering and Trauma

The word *trauma* is being used a lot these days, and it can get watered down, overused, and stripped of its true meaning when people use the term casually or offhandedly. However, the severity of the experience of comprehensive and chronic suffering may truly lead to traumatization. Counselor Darby Strickland defines trauma in this way:

> *Trauma* refers to the emotional, spiritual, and physical disruptions that occur when a person is overwhelmed by extreme suffering. . . . An event may rise to the level of a traumatic experience when it is sudden and unpredictable, involves a threat to life, or is a profound violation of trust. The word *traumatized* also describes a person who is overwhelmed after a series of adverse experiences. . . . Traumatized people often experience a severe disruption in their relationships with God and others because of what has happened.[3]

It's easy to see how comprehensive and chronic suffering can lead to trauma, but some may wonder, What is the relationship between suffering and trauma? Perhaps the simplest way to conceptualize it is to imagine a large circle labeled *suffering*. Within that larger circle of suffering, imagine a smaller circle labeled *trauma*. In other words, not all suffering results in trauma, but all trauma involves suffering. It's also important to note that experiencing trauma does not indicate that a person lacks spiritual maturity. As creatures, we are finite and frail beings, both body and soul.

While the Bible does not use the specific word *trauma*, it does portray deep affliction and the various spiritual, physical, and relational problems that such affliction can produce. Because trauma (or, for those who prefer other terminology, "severe affliction") lies within the broader realm of suffering, God's Word provides hope and help to those who have been traumatized by comprehensive and chronic suffering. But because this smaller circle of trauma has contours and features that are often not present in the larger, more general circle of suffering, biblically wise and nuanced care is imperative for those whose experience has resulted in trauma.

Our Lord Jesus knew how to care for afflicted people. He fulfilled the prophecy of Isaiah: "The Lord God has given me the tongue of those who are taught, that I may know how to sustain with a word him who is weary" (50:4). Jesus knew how to wisely use his words in ways that brought sustenance and strength to the weary. He also fulfilled the prophecy that "a bruised reed he will not break, and a faintly burning wick he will not quench" (42:3). Jesus did not act or speak in ways that crushed the brokenhearted or extinguished the last flicker of hope from the downcast.

It took a long time for me to recognize that my suffering had resulted in trauma. For years, I met with multiple counselors I trusted and respected, but it didn't seem to help very much. I expected myself to just "get over it" and "move on" (and it seemed like that was what other people wanted me to do as well). I berated myself for not being "godlier," for not being "strong" or "faithful" enough in my adversity. But no matter how much I tried to get a handle on my suffering, I didn't make any progress. When the interpretive lens of trauma was introduced to me, so much began to make sense in terms of my internal emotional landscape and my physical bodily responses. I finally felt as though someone were describing my feelings and struggles exactly. I wasn't crazy, stupid, or rebellious. Rather, I had experienced too much, too fast, for too long, with too little support, and I had been pushed to the farthest borders, spiritually and physically, of what I could handle.

Have you found that truths and strategies that enabled you to walk through other types of suffering in the past haven't seemed to address your current experience of comprehensive and chronic suffering? Or have you received general counseling that has proven unhelpful (and perhaps even caused more harm)? If so, looking into biblical counseling resources on trauma, as well as working with a counselor who has experience in this area, could be profoundly helpful.

What About Sin?

Some people might ask what this book has to say about *sin* and its relationship to suffering and sufferers. It's certainly true that all God's people are simultaneously saints, sinners, and sufferers. Suffering never justifies or excuses sin, and sufferers are not sinless people. But the intended focus of this book is to "zoom in" on the experience of suffering to grapple with some of the particular challenges to faith that can occur in deep affliction. While it's true that sometimes we suffer because of our sin, and inevitably we'll sin when we suffer, there are many fine books and other resources to help Christians fight against sin. The purpose of this book, however, is to focus our attention on how to "encourage the fainthearted" and "help the weak" rather than on how to "admonish the idle" (1 Thess. 5:14).

When it comes to suffering and sin, the book of Job teaches us to resist hasty assumptions based on limited information. This book is geared toward those whose suffering seems to fit best within the category of Job-like suffering—people who have spent much time and shed many tears asking the Lord and others what sin may be causing their suffering and can't seem to find an answer, or who labor to discern particular areas of needed growth that their suffering may be intended to produce and come away with no clear answers. It is for these reasons that the sufferer's sin is not a focus in this book.

More to the Story

As one might expect, there's a lot more to my story than what I've shared here. My goal is not to provide an exhaustive, detailed narrative of everything that's happened to me but rather to highlight for readers what it can look and feel like when comprehensive and chronic suffering intrudes into one's life. I'm not writing this book as someone who now has it all "figured out" or who doesn't wrestle with the topics we'll cover. I struggle every day, especially as each year seems to bring a heavier load of health problems.

I've never gotten back to "normal" life but am seeking to adapt over time to the radically different life and circumstances I've been given, doing my best at the opportunities I do have and trying to let go of everything in life that remains out of my grasp. I don't feel like I "fit in" in the normal world of healthy, independent adults and the lives they lead. But I am trying to operate within the story the Lord is writing for me rather than expending my limited energy frantically trying to snatch the pen out of his hand so that I can become the author and write the life story I wish I had. And isn't there a sense in which all of us must do that?

2

MISERABLE COMFORTERS

When I was in college, I experienced my first major heartbreak. It was my first serious dating relationship, and we had both wanted to marry each other. But then one summer evening, it all came crashing down when he unexpectedly broke up with me. Emotionally devastated, I called a friend who was in town taking summer school classes. But she did much more than simply seek to console me over the phone. Minutes later, she showed up at my apartment with her sleeping bag, which she laid on the floor next to my bed to spend the night with me so that I wasn't alone.

Fast forward about ten years later. I was living in California and taking a run one morning before work. Suddenly, I started having severe lower back pain and felt like I was going to pass out. I couldn't make it back to my apartment, so I lay down on the sidewalk next to the road, hoping that someone driving by would see me and help. I lay there and watched several cars drive by without stopping. Finally, a man rolled down his window and asked if I was OK. I told him I couldn't make it home and asked if he could drive me just a few yards to my apartment complex. He replied that he was bringing donuts to a work meeting and didn't have time to help.

Most of us can recount stories when someone helped us in a time of need, as well as stories when no one helped us in a time of need. These opposing experiences reveal an important truth about suffering: What often tips the scales from suffering's being bearable to unbearable is the degree to which we feel seen, heard, supported, helped, and loved by others in our deep distress. Shared suffering is endurable; solitary suffering is unbearable. Not only can a lack of supportive relationships make the suffering seem unbearable, but how people respond (or don't respond) to us can worsen our suffering, pouring salt in an already gaping wound and leading to greater distress and disorientation.

The Bible tells us that belonging to a local body of believers is critical for our spiritual growth and health. We know that we should be active members of our local congregations. We learn the "one another" passages of the New Testament that show us practically how to treat brothers and sisters in Christ. We hear Jesus say that the world will be able to identify Christians by their love for one another (see John 13:35). We read books and articles on suffering in which authors talk about their own personal experiences and say that they would never have made it through their suffering were it not for the love and help they received from people in their churches.

But what happens when that's not what we experience in our suffering? What happens if our suffering is compounded, or even *caused*, by how others respond to us in our darkest hours (or months or years) of need? How are we to make sense of the dissonance between the Bible's teaching and the positive experiences of others in their time of need versus our own negative experiences in our time of need? These are some of the questions that we'll seek to answer in this chapter.

Job's Counselors

If it seems strange to devote a whole chapter to the reality of miserable comforters in a book on suffering, then consider the book of Job. God has given us an entire book devoted to the severe suffering of one human being. And in that book, a dominant thread running through from start to finish is how other people—and often those we'd consider our closest friends—can compound our suffering.

This is not to say that there aren't many godly people and wonderful churches that minister to the sufferers in their midst in wise, sacrificial, loving, Christlike ways. But it is to say that when this doesn't happen, we need help understanding how to interpret our negative experiences and how they relate to what we believe about God, ourselves, and others. To put it another way, the focus in this chapter is not on what *should* happen in the body of Christ but rather on how we can reorient ourselves when things *don't* happen the way they should in the body of Christ.

Before diving in, it's important to note a particularly difficult situation that often arises in comprehensive suffering. When suffering forces people to uproot themselves and move somewhere new, they suddenly lose all their existing community, both in the church and in their other relational spheres. Being thrust into the earthquake of comprehensive suffering while simultaneously losing established relationships and church connections can be a devastating combination.

In such cases, sometimes sufferers trust new people too quickly and disclose information about their circumstances too early in their relationships because they desperately need community and care, especially from the church. This can backfire when sufferers entrust the deeply painful and fragile pieces of their lives into the hands of untested acquaintances who may not have the spiritual maturity to love them well.

Because of these realities, if you have recently relocated and need care and support in your suffering, you may be better served by working with counselors and pastoral staff first. By allowing those who are better equipped to handle the delicate and fragile pieces of your life first, you can be freed to slow down and build trusted relationships with others over time without feeling the pressure and desperation that might lead you to prematurely entrust your story to them.

Five Damaging Responses to Suffering

Miserable comforters tend to have the following five unloving responses to those who are suffering: (1) accusation, (2) aphorisms, (3) abandonment, (4) avoidance, and (5) apathy. We'll begin by exploring each of these responses, the first of which is most displayed in how Job's friends responded to his suffering.

Accusation

Job's friends responded to him primarily with accusations (see, for example, Job 4:7–8; 11:14–17). Because they had no framework for the concept of righteous suffering, they doubled down on the only interpretational grid they had: Good things happen to good people, and bad things happen to bad people. Job was continually worn down in conversation after conversation as his three friends—Eliphaz, Bildad, and Zophar—took turns insisting that Job's circumstances must have been due to sin on his part. If he would only repent, he would be restored. Their erroneous counsel not only failed to help Job; it also may have contributed to the skewed conclusions he began to draw about God's character and God's heart toward him.

Unfortunately, this response to sufferers has stood the test of time, and thousands of years later, many sufferers still experience, to one degree or another, these accusatory responses from others. This happens when the assumption is made that suffering is always a result of one's personal sin, or that suffering always indicates a deficiency in godly character that needs to be developed, or that suffering shouldn't evoke grief or confusion. Accusers often lack compassion for others and their circumstances and, whether consciously or unconsciously, set themselves above sufferers as the ones who are qualified to make definitive judgments about what is happening to them and why. An accusatory response can result from legalism, an inaccurate theology of suffering, a fear of not "knowing the right answer," or an inability to tolerate mystery in the Christian life. Accusatory responses can also happen when someone has a superficial or unbalanced understanding, interpretation, and application of God's Word.

Being accused of sin can be confusing to sufferers because there are often elements of truth in what's being said. They know that they are not sinless. They know that there are always sins they need to repent of. They can start to feel pressure to live up to a "superhuman" (and ultimately superficial) Christianity that admits no weakness, struggle, negative emotions, or doubts, lest their faith or spiritual maturity be called into question. And unfortunately, these accusations can lead sufferers down the wrong path, compounding their miseries when they received condemnation instead of compassion.

Aphorisms

Closely related to the response of accusation is the response of offering aphorisms. This occurs when people launch biblical sound bites at sufferers without attempting to listen, empathize, understand, comfort, help, or weep with them. This approach minimizes suffering, treating it as a superficial problem that can be efficiently remedied with a superficial cure that requires little time, commitment, or relational connection. Verses of Scripture are often extracted from their larger context and indiscriminately lobbed at sufferers.

Unfortunately, such miserable comforters often think they've helped a suffering person because the words that they're speaking come from the Bible. When a sufferer opens up about their grief, pain, loss, or problems, a miserable comforter offering aphorisms may respond with sentiments such as "Paul tells us to rejoice always. How can you rejoice right now in your circumstances?" or "We're supposed to be content with whatever the Lord gives us. In what ways do you need to repent of your discontent?" Maybe they simply say, "You just need to trust the Lord," or "Jesus is enough." Or maybe they ask, "How can you suffer well right now?"

The problem here is not so much the content of these statements. These responses might be appropriate and accurate in certain contexts and circumstances. But Proverbs warns us, "If one gives an answer before he hears, it is his folly and shame" (Prov. 18:13). We should do a lot of listening and work hard to understand a sufferer before jumping in with words that may be completely inaccurate and unhelpful to their situation. The aphoristic responses listed in the preceding paragraph are just biblical enough to make sufferers feel guilty and assume they must be doing something wrong, but they're unbiblically applied and function more like a madman's knife wounds than a wise surgeon's healing scalpel.

Proverbs also cautions us about how we respond to those who are afflicted: "Whoever sings songs to a heavy heart is like one who takes off a garment on a cold day, and like vinegar on soda" (25:20). The danger of aphorisms—even biblical ones—is that they can contradict the wisdom God has given to us regarding the timing of our words for those who are hurting.

Abandonment

Another way that people can respond to sufferers is by abandoning them. This occurs when people who were once close to a sufferer pull away from them in their suffering and essentially discontinue the relationship. We can't judge why another person has withdrawn from us if they haven't told us directly, but it hurts nonetheless. It may be that those who abandon relationships lack maturity and don't know how to walk with someone who is suffering. It may be that they are selfish and only interested in easy and fun relationships. It may be that they really do care but are terrified of doing or saying the wrong thing, so they pull away. Or it may be that they are overwhelmed in their own lives or experiencing suffering we can't see from the outside. In any case, the real or perceived abandonment is deeply painful to sufferers who long for the presence of others in their affliction.

Avoidance

Avoidance is another common response to suffering people. It's a milder version of abandonment in which people don't totally withdraw, but they hold a sufferer at arm's length and reduce their interactions with them. As with abandonment, a person may do this for a variety of reasons, including immaturity, selfishness, fear, overwhelm, or their own suffering. It can be disorienting for sufferers, though, as it leaves them with many confusing and unanswered questions.

Both abandonment and avoidance, whether real or perceived, can fill sufferers with a sense of shame. They might wonder, Did I do something wrong? Am I unworthy of care and support? Does this person not value our relationship as much as I do? Does this person still want to be my friend? Seeking answers to these questions can be difficult. After all, what if we ask them and find out that our friend doesn't value the relationship as much as we do or that they don't want to continue the friendship? In a time when sufferers most need support, they can get turned around and confused within this interpersonal landscape.

Sensing that people are avoiding us can also make us unsure about how to interact with others in the body of Christ, whether they are people we already know or new people we meet. We can second-guess ourselves, asking questions such as "Did I share too much? Did I share too little? Should I not be honest about my pain and my needs? Should I just try to get through this myself without bothering anyone?" The extra toll that this takes on sufferers can be mentally, emotionally, and even physically depleting.

Apathy

A fifth way that miserable comforters can respond poorly to sufferers is with apathy, which literally means "without feeling" or "without suffering." Apathetic responses occur when people either remain unmoved by the suffering of others or feel badly for sufferers but fail to turn that compassion into helpful action on the sufferer's behalf. When we feel badly for someone but fail to engage with them in helpful ways, we can often fool ourselves into thinking that we've done something when we haven't done anything at all. I know I've been guilty of this. I've felt compassion toward someone who is suffering and thought about something I could do to help them. Though I never actually followed through with action, I told myself that I had somehow helped the person by feeling compassion when I hadn't done anything for their benefit.

But compassion must spring forward into action if it's going to benefit another person. Receiving an apathetic response is particularly painful when sufferers have done their due diligence to make their situation and their needs known. In other words, sometimes sufferers don't receive the support and help they need because, for whatever reason, they haven't truly made others aware of their needs. But when they have done so and not received a response, it's both painful and scary to be left to handle things on their own.

Acknowledging the Hurt

If you have experienced any of these responses in your suffering, you can be comforted and encouraged to know that you are not alone. Such hurtful responses were a major part of Job's experience as well. When they are part of your own story, it does not mean that you are unlovable or unworthy of care from others. It does not necessarily mean that you have done anything wrong; rather, it may be simply a part of your suffering that you must honestly acknowledge, grieve, and process with the Lord (and maybe with a trusted friend, counselor, or pastor as well).

It's probably safe to say that most of us have experienced at least one of these responses, regardless of the degree of suffering we've faced. But the more comprehensive and chronic your suffering is, the more likely it is that you'll experience one or all of these unhelpful responses. And when you do, you may need help knowing what to do.

Sometimes people respond to sufferers in one of the five ways outlined above because they lack spiritual maturity and are unable to bear the weight of heavy things. In his commentary on the book of Ecclesiastes, author Zack Eswine notes,

> Our friends and family can mishandle us. When we experience a circumstance under the sun that they sought to avoid all of their lives, they sting us with their theological and relational unpreparedness. They underestimate and mismanage what such times actually require of us. Yesterday the leg bones broke. Today, hunched on crutches we turtle and snail along. Rather than slow down or ice the swelling with us, they run on ahead shouting back to us

with cheerleading voices that the brisk walk or the long jog will do us some good.[1]

In other words, people often respond poorly to a sufferer because they're afraid that the same kinds of things might happen to them. After all, if a faithful Christian can experience affliction and loss of such epic proportions, who is to say that the same thing won't happen to them too? And sometimes, in the attempt to convince themselves that the same kinds of things won't ever happen to them, they blame the sufferer and find fault where there is none to mentally assure themselves that they are immune to the other person's experience.

Of course, a sufferer's own sin might encourage such unhelpful responses, though they're probably not aware of it. We want to avoid the extremes. On one hand, we don't want to heap condemnation on ourselves and try to figure out what we're doing wrong when it's possible that we haven't done anything to provoke an unhelpful reaction. But on the other hand, we don't want to assume that the problem is always with other people when we may be blind to ways in which we have contributed to or caused our pain. This is where a wise, loving, and trusted counselor, pastor, or friend can help us examine the situation and gain clarity, enabling us to free ourselves from false guilt or repent of actual sin.

When the Church Doesn't Act Like the Church

Most of us know how relationships in the body of Christ are *supposed* to function. Any shortcomings may be less obvious to us at times when we find ourselves in relative ease.

But in the face of comprehensive and chronic suffering, the shortcomings and failures of the body of Christ can become glaringly and painfully obvious.

Romans 12:9–21 gives us a glorious picture of a properly functioning church body. This body is characterized by showing brotherly affection, helping those in need, practicing hospitality, and weeping with those who weep. We read in Acts 2:42–47 of the unity and camaraderie of the early church. We remember Jesus's own words that "by this all people will know that you are my disciples, if you have love for one another" (John 13:35). And we see the apostle John echo Jesus's teaching when he says,

> By this we know love, that he laid down his life for us, and we ought to lay down our lives for the brothers and sisters. But if anyone has the world's goods and sees his brother in need, yet closes his heart against him, how does God's love abide in him? Little children, let us not love in word or talk but in deed and in truth. (1 John 3:16–18)

But what happens when that isn't a sufferer's experience? Not receiving assistance from other believers may be especially difficult for those who are without a spouse or family to help them financially and practically or to provide companionship and encouragement. What happens when the family of God doesn't act like family at all? What happens when those who are most vulnerable, and most in need of care and help, are the most overlooked and neglected? What happens when someone's community group isn't a community at all, or when their care group is too busy to care?

This reality isn't foreign to the Bible. It may seem to be the case, since we tend to focus on the beautiful vision of what God (and we) desire the church to be. And when our experience doesn't line up with what Scripture calls the church to be, we may be tempted to think that Scripture isn't true after all, because our own experience negates what is laid out in its pages.

But the truth is that Scripture actually does describe breakdowns and heartaches within the family of God— perhaps more than we might realize at first glance. For example, the same church that had all things in common in Acts 4 also overlooked some of the widows in its daily distribution of aid (see Acts 6). The apostle Paul tells the Corinthian church that they have received grace from God and are in every way enriched in him (see 1 Cor. 1:4–5). Yet he also admonishes this same church for the divisions in their midst, their sexual immorality, their selfish prioritization of their personal rights at the expense of others' spiritual well-being, and the distinctions they created between rich and poor as they partook of the Lord's Supper (see 1 Cor. 1; 3; 5; 8; 11).

The apostle Paul himself experienced wounds from the churches and believers with whom he loved, served, and worshiped the Lord. His friend Demas turned away from him and the ministry (see 2 Tim. 4:10). Alexander the coppersmith did him great harm (see v. 14). No one came to support him or stand with him during his first defense; instead, they all deserted him (see v. 16). This is the same Paul who ministered to hundreds if not thousands of people. This is the same Paul who littered his letters with the names of friends and beloved fellow workers. But in his moment of need, everyone who could have been there for him didn't show up. They all deserted him. Sufferers who have shared these kinds of experiences are not alone.

We can see how disillusionment with the church can arise when negative experiences in the body of Christ add to our suffering. Yet it's important to remember that Jesus purchased the church with his own blood (see Acts 20:28). The church, while deeply flawed, is precious to God. And while there may be valid reasons to leave a particular local church, we must take care not to abandon the church as a whole when we are suffering but instead to extend patience to fellow brothers and sisters who may in their hearts desire to help but in practice still need time to learn how to do so.

How Jesus Was Treated by His Friends

As we look at the apostle Paul's experience, we can't help but think of someone else when we hear that "all deserted" him. One greater than even the apostle Paul knows the pain of his friends' not standing with him in his time of greatest need. He was "a living stone rejected by men but in the sight of God chosen and precious" (1 Peter 2:4). As we consider the experience of being hurt more than helped by the church in our suffering, let's fix our gaze on the story of our Lord Jesus Christ.

- *Accusation*: In Mark 3:21, we see those closest to Jesus wrongly accuse him of being out of his mind.
- *Aphorisms*: When Jesus candidly told his disciples about his impending suffering and death, Peter

rebuked him, saying that such things would never happen (see Matt. 16:22). Peter was seeking to cover over uncomfortable, painful truths and thus responded inappropriately.

- *Abandonment*: As Jesus made his mission increasingly clear, "many of his disciples turned back and no longer walked with him" (John 6:66). When the soldiers came to arrest Jesus in the garden of Gethsemane, "all the disciples left him and fled" (Matt. 26:56).
- *Avoidance*: During Jesus's trial at the high priest's house, Peter stayed at a distance in the courtyard, afraid to be recognized as one of Jesus's followers (see John 18:15–27).
- *Apathy*: In Luke 22, Jesus told his disciples that he was going to be betrayed. Instead of responding to him with love and care, they got into an argument about who was the greatest. Similarly, in Mark 10, when Jesus predicted his humiliation and death, James and John asked to sit with him in his glory rather than responding with loving care to what Jesus had shared with them.

Job Forgives His Foolish Friends

It's fascinating to see how Job's friends are involved in the conclusion of his story. We might be tempted to think that once God had appeared to Job, and once Job beheld God in a way that restored and strengthened his relationship with him, the friends would simply exit stage left and disappear from the story. But that's not what happens.

Instead, before he doubles Job's original blessings, God requires something of him: He must pray for the Lord to forgive his friends. This part of the story tends to be under-emphasized in studies or sermons about Job, but it's a crucial message for the sufferer. As part of maintaining a right relationship with the Lord, as well as part of their healing in severe suffering, sufferers must forgive foolish friends whose accusations have been ungodly and whose aphorisms, abandonment, avoidance, and apathy have compounded their sorrows.

We see similar prayers for forgiveness from the martyr Stephen, the apostle Paul, and our Lord Jesus. When Stephen was being stoned, he cried out, "Lord, do not hold this sin against them" (Acts 7:60). When Paul was abandoned by his friends, he exclaimed in his letter to Timothy, "May it not be charged against them!" (2 Tim. 4:16). And when Jesus was crucified, he said, "Father, forgive them, for they know not what they do" (Luke 23:34).

This doesn't mean that sufferers can't or shouldn't have honest conversations with people about how they've been hurt by them. It doesn't mean that crimes perpetrated against people shouldn't be reported to the appropriate authorities. It doesn't mean that we shouldn't exercise wisdom in the extent to which we engage or interact with certain people. But it does mean that sin is always crouching at the door ready to consume us, even (or especially) in our suffering.

By extending forgiveness, sufferers unburden their hearts from bitterness and hand over the gavel to the only true Judge, refusing to allow their suffering to be made worse by responding sinfully. It may take a lot of time, tears, and trusted counsel, and that's okay. Over time, this forms us into the image of the ultimate Job, our Lord Jesus Christ, who cried out in the days of his flesh to his Father, "Forgive them, for they know not what they do."

Zack Eswine comments that Job "wailed and groaned in the midst of unexplained misery, amid the presence of God's silence and the absence of a friend's love."[2] Job says this in his affliction:

> [God] has put my brothers far from me,
>> and those who knew me are wholly estranged from me.
> My relatives have failed me,
>> my close friends have forgotten me. (Job 19:13–14)

> My breath is strange to my wife,
>> and I am a stench to the children of my own mother.
>> (v. 17)

> All my intimate friends abhor me,
>> and those whom I loved have turned against me. (v. 19)

How might Job's story have been different if he had experienced his suffering in the context of compassionate, wise, and loving relationships with his friends? There's no way to know for sure. But we do know that because his suffering was compounded rather than comforted by the words and actions of his friends, we are not alone if this is our experience in suffering too.

In that sense, sufferers are in good company as they look to the story of Job and map their experience onto his: a believer dearly loved by God who nevertheless did *not* experience the blessing of faithful and wise friends in his deepest affliction and his time of greatest need.

A Strange Twist in the Story of Job

We know how the book of Job ends. God appears to Job. Job repents of speaking words without knowledge. God vindicates Job. Job forgives his friends. God restores and doubles Job's fortune and blessings. But there's something else that happens in Job 42. It's rarely talked about in books or sermons, but it's vital to our discussion of miserable comforters and our struggle to understand why other Christians often aren't there for us in our suffering.

Tucked away in one verse in Job 42, we read this: "Then came to [Job] all his brothers and sisters and all who had known him before, and ate bread with him in his house. And they showed him sympathy and comforted him for all the evil [or disaster] that the Lord had brought upon him. And each of them gave him a piece of money and a ring of gold" (v. 11). This verse should make us stop and scratch our heads.

At the book's conclusion, everyone who had known Job before his suffering finally showed up. But where had they been during all the months of his suffering? We learn in this verse that Job apparently had much family and many friends out there. Why, then, did none of them come to him in his time of need? And why instead did the only friends who came to Job turn out to be miserable comforters who only made things worse and failed to represent God's truth and grace in his unimaginable suffering?

The questions continue. *Now* Job experiences fellowship around a table of food with his loved ones? *Now* Job is shown sympathy and comfort by all these people? And *now* Job receives tangible, physical help through their gifts of money and gold? Where was all this when Job needed it most? And why is he receiving it now, when, in theory, he doesn't really need it like he did during his deepest affliction? Believe it or not, this little verse tucked away in the last chapter of the book can provide perspective and stability for sufferers who are struggling alone amidst miserable comforters and a lack of support. Let's see how this is the case.

When we look at Job 42 and see the abundance of comfort and support that Job received from his family and friends after his testing was complete, it almost seems as though the comfort that Job could have received from others was actively withheld from him during his suffering. Why? Perhaps because the presence of miserable comforters and the absence of life-giving comforters was itself a major part of Job's suffering, trial, and testing.

In other words, if Job had experienced life-giving comforters, then the parameters of the test outlined in Job 1 would have been violated. In that case, Job would have still been receiving blessings from God and the mediated presence of God through his godly friends. Therefore, Satan could have argued that Job was still only following God because of what he gained from God—in this case, the presence of godly, loving friends.

Naming and acknowledging this aspect of testing can bring comfort to those who are suffering like Job. It helps to protect us from the shame that comes from believing that our lack of godly comforters somehow directly correlates to our worth as human beings. But being unloved by others amid comprehensive and chronic suffering does not mean that you are inherently unlovable any more than Job's experience meant that he was inherently unlovable. Therefore, you need not find it completely bewildering if you, too, lack care from others.

It may well be that for reasons beyond your understanding, not revealed to you by God, you are also experiencing a test to prove that your worship of him does not depend on whether or not he ordains favorable circumstances for your life.

Of course, this isn't the only possible reason why relational breakdowns might be present in your deep suffering. It doesn't mean that you might not be contributing in some way to these difficulties. And it doesn't mean that you shouldn't continue seeking the support of godly friends and helpers. But it is a hopeful truth if you are tempted toward self-condemnation and shame when you've faced any of the five responses outlined here.

Finding a Way Forward

Since this experience of miserable comforters is so painful and disorienting, let's close this chapter with some additional practical advice for when miserable comforters are wounding you.

Honestly acknowledge to the Lord and others how you've been impacted by miserable comforters. This is not a license to gossip but rather an invitation to seek reconciliation with those who have hurt you. If it's not best or wise to discuss your hurt with those people directly, work with a counselor, pastor, or friend who will grieve your mistreatment with you, allow you to express your pain to them, and offer wise counsel regarding how you might respond to the wounds of miserable comforters.

Consider whether unreasonable expectations for others have played a role in your hurt. Since this can be very difficult for us to assess on our own, this is best done alongside a trusted counselor, pastor, or friend.

Employ wisdom in who you are transparent with and who you seek help from. Some believers lack the spiritual maturity and wisdom to walk well with sufferers. If a Christian can't handle the hard words spoken by Job, Jeremiah, or others in Scripture, then they probably aren't ready to handle your hard words either.

Recognize how being treated poorly by others in your suffering can help you be more thoughtful and wise in your own interactions with suffering people. Often those who have been wounded know how to minister to others with grace and truth that is life-giving and truly comforts the downcast.

3

THE ANCIENT SERPENT

I once watched a documentary in which a con artist posing as an MI5 agent in the 1990s convinced three college students that the Irish Republican Army was after them.[1] They were manipulated into going on the run with him, hiding in various "safe houses" and extracting money from their families to pay for the costs associated with "witness protection."

One of these women lost ten years of her life to this diabolical deception. She was cut off from her family and friends for a decade. She didn't get to graduate from college or start a career. Instead, she worked odd jobs set up for her by the "MI5 agent" and had to turn over all her wages to him. She had no access to her personal identification cards, passport, or bank account. She wore down her parents to the point that they eventually handed her entire inheritance over to the "agent." For ten years, she had no friends, family, money, personal agency, or freedom. At some points, she was left locked in rooms for days, completely at the mercy of the "agent" to bring her food or let her out.

Of course, this man was not who he claimed to be. He was not an MI5 agent invested in her well-being, safety, and protection but an evil, sociopathic con man willing to destroy not only her life but the lives of many other people in his lust to satisfy his own desires. He was able to keep her in this kind of bondage, when in theory she could have escaped at any point, because of the nature of the deception: He was a bad man who was destroying her, but he posed as a good man who was saving her.

The Ultimate Con Artist

Watching that documentary filled me with empathy for the woman who'd lost ten years of her life to a liar. But it also did something else. It provided a clear picture of what Jesus meant when he called Satan "the father of lies." Speaking to the Jewish religious leaders who opposed him, Jesus said, "You are of your father the devil, and your will is to do your father's desires. He was a murderer from the beginning, and does not stand in the truth, because there is no truth in him. When he lies, he speaks out of his own character, for he is a liar and the father of lies" (John 8:44).

Satan is the ultimate con man. Human con artists offer merely a faint reflection of the deception, arrogance, and malice that is in Satan. As I watched this woman's story unfold, I was struck with a penetrating question for myself and my story: To what extent over the past ten years of my suffering had believing the lies of Satan heaped greater agony and confusion onto an already difficult story? Was I, too, being conned without realizing it?

Those who are living with comprehensive and chronic suffering are especially susceptible to Satan's attacks. After all, the easiest targets are those who are the weakest, the most worn down, the most mentally and physically exhausted. This also connects to our discussion of miserable comforters in chapter 2. The more that sufferers are surrounded by mature fellow believers who meaningfully support them, the less susceptible they tend to be to Satan's temptations. But the more that people find themselves alone and isolated—whether due to health limitations, caretaking responsibilities, financial obligations, remote living situations, or breakdowns in caring and supportive relationships in their churches—the more likely it is that Satan can get his lies to land in their hearts and attack their faith. Paul Tripp notes, "[Satan's] lies are meant to damage and weaken our faith so that on the other side of our suffering (if there is another side) we will not love and serve [God] as we once did."[2]

We might say that, in his attempts to destroy our faith in the Lord, Satan is an artist. He sits before the easel with palette and brush in hand. His subject is God himself. He's had a long time to perfect his craft, and he knows what will induce people to buy his work. God is good, but Satan paints him as cruel and uncaring. God is close to his children, but Satan paints him as distant. God desires our best, but Satan paints him as desiring our worst. God gives good gifts, but Satan paints him as withholding good gifts. God ordains grief and pain, but Satan paints him as delighting in our pain and motivated by a desire to see us suffer. God is compassionate, but Satan paints him as harsh. God's ways are worth obeying, but Satan paints his ways as foolish and unsatisfying.

Satan is a con artist. He sells us caricatures of God and seeks to convince us that each one is an accurate representation of reality. Why does he do this, and what is he after?

What Satan Wants

Have you ever stopped to ask, "What does Satan want more than anything else?" After all, if we have an enemy (and the Bible says that we do), wouldn't it be in our best interest to understand what he ultimately wants? Scripture doesn't leave us to guess the answers. Satan wants two things more than anything else: (1) to receive the glory that God alone deserves, and (2) to destroy the faith of the people of God. As such, he exploits our suffering by seeking to use it in ways that aim to destroy faith in God and detract from the glory of God. The fact that Satan seeks to use *sin* to draw us away from the Lord is often discussed in the evangelical world. But for some reason, much less attention is given to how Satan seeks to use *suffering* to accomplish the same ends. Because of this imbalance, you may be ill-prepared to identify the schemes of Satan in your affliction.

We see Satan pursuing these two goals in the first chapter of the book of Job. Interestingly, it was not initially Satan who targeted Job. God was the one who said to Satan, "Have you considered my servant Job?" (1:8). Satan argues that Job fears God only because of the blessings that Job has received from him. He further predicts that if God were to allow everything to be taken away from Job, he would curse God to his face. This cycle of conversations occurs again in chapter 2, this time regarding Job's health.

There are two beings working behind the scenes in Job's life: God and Satan. Each was involved in what happened, and each had specific purposes and goals. Part of walking through comprehensive and chronic suffering includes making sure that we clearly understand how God and Satan are both involved, as well as the purposes and goals they each have.

The Face Behind the Malice

Sometimes, in our good desire to emphasize the truth of God's sovereignty, we can unwittingly conflate God's sovereignty and Satan's malice in how we communicate about suffering. When that happens, we worsen the suffering that people experience by inaccurately conveying what the Bible teaches. Here's what I mean: When God's sovereignty (a critically important reality) is treated as though it's the *only* reality at play in our suffering, an unfortunate consequence is that malice—an intention or desire to do evil—can also be attributed to God along with his sovereignty. In other words, an incomplete view of Satan's involvement in suffering can confuse sufferers by wrongly putting God's face on Satan's malice.

When we feel malevolence and hostility directed toward us as we suffer, there's a sense in which that's true. In a class on suffering at my church, one of the participants shared how the specific and targeted nature of his trials often felt gratuitous. But if we think that this spiteful animosity is coming from God, we will end up in dark and dangerous places. This is a critical distinction to make when we struggle to see God for who he truly is in the midst of our pain. Let's consider how Scripture speaks of both Satan's malicious intent and God's gracious intent in our suffering.

It's clear that Satan's intentions for Job were malicious. By afflicting Job in the ways that he did, Satan sought to

(1) detract from God's glory by leading one of his followers to turn away from him and curse him when blessings were taken away and (2) destroy Job's faith and relationship to God. Jesus says of Satan, "The thief comes only to steal and kill and destroy" (John 10:10). Satan sought to steal God's glory, kill Job's faith, and destroy the relationship between God and Job. And he has the same goals for every believer facing suffering.

Many passages in Scripture show Satan's involvement in our suffering. For example, when Jesus healed a woman who had been physically bent over for eighteen years, he said, "Ought not this woman, a daughter of Abraham whom Satan bound for eighteen years, be loosed from this bond on the Sabbath day?" (Luke 13:16). Jesus attributes her physical suffering to the malice of Satan. In Acts 10, Peter remarks on Jesus's earthly ministry by saying, "He went about doing good and healing all who were oppressed by the devil" (v. 38). Peter here attributes physical suffering to the oppression of the devil. In Revelation 2, Jesus tells the church at Smyrna, "Do not fear what you are about to suffer. Behold, the devil is about to throw some of you into prison, that you may be tested, and for ten days you will have tribulation" (v. 10).

Satan can be involved in the many different types of suffering that believers experience. His motivation is always the same: hatred of God and of all who belong to God. And his purpose is always the same: the destruction of our faith and the destruction of our relationship with God. Therefore, if we sense an acute hatred directed toward us in our suffering, we're not crazy. But we mustn't conclude that this malice is coming from God, because it's not.

How Satan Sounds

We know that believers battle against a world that is hostile to God, against temptations and assaults of Satan and his minions, and against our own fallen flesh and sinful desires. It's probably unrealistic to think that we can always place our battles neatly into one category or another, as though they were discrete or unrelated. But Scripture does inform us of Satan's methods to help us identify them in our own lives.

In the garden of Eden, Satan came to Eve in the form of a serpent. He first asked her, "Did God actually say, 'You shall not eat of any tree in the garden'?" (Gen. 3:1). His initial approach was to create doubt and distrust of what God had said and, by extension, doubt and distrust of God himself. It's as though Satan saw a tiny crack of potential opportunity, and he didn't hesitate to drive in a wedge to see how far he could separate Eve from her God. He assured her, "You will not surely die. For God knows that when you eat of it your eyes will be opened, and you will be like God, knowing good and evil" (vv. 4–5).

Doubt of God's words, doubt of God's wisdom, doubt of God's care, and doubt of God's goodwill. These are the tools Satan used, and they're the same tools he uses today. Like the con artist posing as an MI5 agent, the devil sought to persuade Eve to start listening to a different voice—his voice—and convince her to believe that voice above all others. He does the same with us. He tries to convince us that God really doesn't love us or care about us, or that it's abnormal or wrong to experience deep affliction as Christians. He takes advantage of our weakness and confusion in our suffering. Sometimes we don't even recognize that the voice we're listening to is his. He seeks to separate us from God and to convince us that God's will really isn't in our best interest. Paul Tripp writes, "The central lie of Satan to all God's suffering children comes in the form of this question: 'Where is your God now?' The lie embedded in this question is that our suffering is clear evidence that we have been forsaken by God. And if God would leave us to such travail, how is he worthy of our trust? It is a direct attack on the truthfulness and goodness of God."[3]

Many of the hard questions that we're covering in this book have biblical answers that Satan loves to pervert. He desires that we embrace a worldview in which the answers to our genuine and pained questions about God and his ways will lead us to conclude that God is a horrible monster rather than a loving Father.

Therefore, if you are living with comprehensive and chronic suffering, it's important to recognize that Satan always tries to exploit your weakness and vulnerability, and who is weaker and more vulnerable than someone enduring heavy suffering, especially in isolation? We need to recognize Satan's role in our suffering—not so that we are terrified of him but so that we can wisely assess the reality of our situation and respond appropriately.

Why This Matters

While the idea may seem counterintuitive, it can actually be encouraging to recognize Satan's involvement in your suffering. After all, comprehensive and chronic suffering can result in much mental confusion and anguish, making it hard to see clearly. Things become hazy and blur together, and it can be difficult to distinguish one thing from another. A proper understanding of Satan's involvement in suffering can clarify the battlefield and help you avoid falling into the Enemy's traps.

We've already noted that it's not always possible to fully parse out what has to do with our own flesh and what has to do with the devil, since they're often intertwined. But there is practical spiritual value in acknowledging that the hard thoughts about God that may be ricocheting in your head are not completely manufactured by your own flesh. Rather, Satan is exploiting your suffering, watering tiny seeds of doubt about God's character, and doing everything he can to paint an ugly caricature of God in the hopes that you will ultimately turn away from him. In his commentary on the book of Job, Christopher Ash notes,

> It is not so much that Job is on the battlefield; he is the battlefield. The battle for the soul of Job is fought out in his struggles as the monster tears at his life. It is a dark warfare. Satan fills Job's mind with images of despair, darkness, death, and futility. Job is taken through the valley of the shadow of death. He is taken there as a believer suffering for his faith. . . . Every morning we ought to wake up and say to ourselves, "There is a vicious, dark spiritual battle being waged over me today."[4]

Knowledge of Satan's involvement in our suffering can empower us. After all, if a sinister, anti-God force is tangled up in our hard thoughts about God, then we're caught up in something much bigger than our own pain, confusion, and doubts. Satan is seeking to lure us away from God, and we have an opportunity to resist his evil agenda. We have an opportunity to reject his lies, even amid our unanswered questions about God. It brings nobility, honor, and dignity to our suffering to know that as we continue to cling to the Lord and refuse to curse him, like Job, we have the opportunity to display to all the heavenly host—God, Satan, angels, and demons—that God's Word is true and that he is worthy of our trust, even when we're in the midst of deeply painful circumstances and deeply anguished questions about who he is and what he is up to in our lives.

Jesus, the Second Adam

Of course, it would be foolish to believe that mere humans can go head-to-head with Satan in their own strength. We can't do this under even the best of circumstances, as is abundantly clear in Adam and Eve's succumbing to Satan's temptations in a beautiful garden sanctuary before indwelling sin even existed. And if we can't do this under the best of circumstances, we certainly can't do it in the face of deep and ongoing suffering. But the good news for Christians is that we are united to the one who can: our Lord Jesus Christ.

Jesus's temptation by Satan in the wilderness followed a pattern similar to Adam and Eve's temptation in Genesis 3—only this time, Satan lost. In Luke 4, Satan came to Jesus in the wilderness to tempt him. In every temptation, Jesus did not listen to Satan's voice.

At the heart of all these temptations was Satan's attempt to sway Jesus from perfect commitment to and unity with his Father and his Father's will. Every time Satan tempted him to go rogue, Jesus refused to allow a wedge to separate him and the Father, his will and the Father's will. They remained in perfect unity and harmony. Nothing that Satan said or did could dissuade Jesus from clinging to the truths of God's Word or from submitting in dependence to the Father's plan of redemption, despite the fact that fulfilling that plan would bring Jesus great affliction.

Because of Jesus's perfect righteousness, not just in his wilderness temptations but throughout his entire thirty-three-year life as a man on this earth, he has opened a way for all temptation-yielders and sinners to be reconciled to God. Because he succeeded where Adam, Eve, and every human being since the fall have failed, he is the only one who can satisfy God's righteous requirements for mankind (see 1 Tim. 2:5). By placing our faith in Jesus as the one through whom we can receive the forgiveness of sins, righteousness, and reconciliation with God, we are united to Christ and indwelt with his Spirit.

This all means that there is forgiveness for our failures, mercy for our weakness, and power for transformation. It means that we battle Satan not in our own strength but in the strength of Christ (which will still often feel like weakness to us). The Son of God came to destroy the works of the devil (see 1 John 3:8), and someday he will destroy the devil himself (see Rev. 20:10).

Not only that, but the ascended Jesus who lives to make intercession for his people prays that our faith would endure. Before his betrayal and arrest, Jesus said to Peter,

> Simon, Simon, behold, Satan demanded to have you, that he might sift you like wheat, but I have prayed for you that your faith may not fail. And when you have turned again, strengthen your brothers. (Luke 22:31–32)

Despite Peter's denial of Jesus, he was restored, and his faith was sustained, because Jesus sustained him. He will do the same for all those who are united to him by faith.

Battle Plan

How can we take the truths we've learned in this chapter and put them into practice in our daily lives as we face the attacks of the devil? A straightforward framework to follow is *recognize* and *resist*. Because chronic and comprehensive suffering can be so physically, mentally, and emotionally draining, simple tools can be helpful.

Recognize

When the apostle Paul writes to the Corinthian church about a matter of church discipline, he explains that he has taken certain actions "so that we would not be outwitted by Satan; for we are *not ignorant of his designs*" (2 Cor. 2:11). And the apostle Peter writes this to suffering believers: "Be sober-minded; be watchful. Your adversary the devil prowls around like a roaring lion, seeking someone to devour" (1 Peter 5:8). Therefore, our first step is to *recognize* the realities of what Scripture says about the devil and his assaults on God's people. We must remember that Satan seeks to do to us what he sought to do to Peter: to sift us like wheat and cause our faith to fail (see Luke 22:31).

We must recognize this not occasionally in the abstract but rather daily in real time amid the trials that come our way. For example, when our circumstances seem to be getting better, only to be followed by successive waves of new suffering piled on top of one another, we might be tempted to think, "God is really against me," "God doesn't want me to have a moment of peace or happiness," or "God loves to afflict me." But when we remember what Scripture says about God and about Satan, we can stop ourselves and say instead, "This is a snare of the devil designed to misrepresent God and destroy my faith." Simply recognizing what's going on is, as they say, half the battle.

Resist

Once we have recognized what's taking place, our next step is to *resist*. First Peter 5:9 says, "Resist [Satan], firm in your faith, knowing that the same kinds of suffering are being experienced by your brotherhood throughout the world." Meanwhile, James 4:7 tells us, "Resist the devil, and he will flee from you." There are many ways to resist Satan, so we'll consider just three: *pray, put on,* and *praise.*

Pray. The good news is that a long and detailed prayer isn't needed; quite the opposite, in fact. Jesus provided the perfect prayer for us when he taught the disciples using what we call "the Lord's Prayer." Though we're used to seeing Matthew 6:13 say, "Deliver us from evil," the Greek phrase used here can also be translated as "Deliver us from the evil one"—in other words, Satan. In the moment of attack, and all the moments after that, we can pray to our heavenly Father, "Lord, deliver me from the Evil One. Help me recognize his assaults, and help me resist him and his lies through the truth of your Word."

Put on the armor of God. Paul writes to the church at Ephesus,

> Put on the whole armor of God, that you may be able to stand against the schemes of the devil. For we do not wrestle

against flesh and blood, but against the rulers, against the authorities, against the cosmic powers over this present darkness, against the spiritual forces of evil in the heavenly places. Therefore take up the whole armor of God, that you may be able to withstand in the evil day, and having done all, to stand firm. Stand therefore, having fastened on the belt of truth, and having put on the breastplate of righteousness, and, as shoes for your feet, having put on the readiness given by the gospel of peace. In all circumstances take up the shield of faith, with which you can extinguish all the flaming darts of the evil one; and take the helmet of salvation, and the sword of the Spirit, which is the word of God, praying at all times in the Spirit, with all prayer and supplication. (Eph. 6:11–18)

Though this is a familiar passage of Scripture, we can often forget it in our day-to-day difficulties. But it's crucial for those experiencing comprehensive and chronic suffering to keep these truths front of mind for daily warfare. As we do so, we are reminded that though we are here on earth, we wrestle against the spiritual forces of evil in the heavenly realm. We resist them in the ways our Lord instructs us to by

- rejecting Satan's lies and replacing them with God's truth;
- remembering that we are counted righteous because of our faith in Christ and his righteousness, meaning that we are now beloved children of God;
- recalling that the good news of the gospel is that we are now at peace with God and no longer his enemies;
- declaring our faith in God's Word rather than allowing our faith to erode;

- proactively using God's Word to counter Satan's attacks; and
- praying to the Father, through the Son, in the Holy Spirit.

In all these ways, we resist the devil.

Praise God. When we remember that Satan's main goals are to detract from God's glory and destroy God's people, we can use his designs in our suffering to produce the exact *opposite* of what he wants. When we sing praises to the Lord amid our affliction, we testify to God's glory and fortify our faith. What Satan wants to use against us, we can use as an opportunity to do what he hates. This is satisfying. Rather than cursing God and abandoning our faith, we can use the suffering to declare that our God is worthy of our worship, no matter what, and that he is worthy of our faith—not because of what our lives look like but because of who he is.

Sufferers can take heart: "The God of peace will soon crush Satan under your feet" (Rom. 16:20). The God whom we struggle to hold on to is holding on to us. He will preserve us through our pain, confusion, and doubt, even while we are struggling to believe that his Word is true when our circumstances appear to scream the opposite. There is a cosmic battle taking place, and we are in it. Therefore, our suffering matters. And one day, Satan will be crushed not only under our Lord's feet but under our feet as well—all because we are united to Christ and share in his victory.

4

THE GOD WHO IS

If we believe that God is for us and with us in our suffering, we can make it through anything. But if we lose the assurance that he is for us and with us—perhaps even wondering if he's actively against us—then despair quickly sets in. After all, if the only One who really matters is no longer on our side, what hope do we have as we live each day with comprehensive and chronic suffering? Suffering is unbearable without the assurance that we are in a right relationship with God and are the recipients of his fatherly care. Yet suffering can also tempt us to doubt what we once firmly believed and make hazy things that once seemed so clear in brighter days.

Job himself experienced a painful dissonance between his understanding of God and his catastrophic circumstances. We can even see this reality through the meaning of Job's name. While its linguistic etymology is uncertain, it was originally a two-syllable word, *i-yob*. "There seems to be a play on Job's name; twice he says that God counts him as an enemy (*oyeb*), so the folk etymology would be something like 'enemy' or 'hostile.'"[1] If this is the correct interpretation, it illustrates very well the challenges that people facing comprehensive and chronic suffering can experience in their relationship with God. This is, in fact, the worst part of suffering, as we begin to wonder, Does God see me as his enemy?

There is no deeper affliction than the agony of soul we experience when we start wondering if God is not for us but against us. We thought that God was our friend, but in our crushing affliction, we start to wonder if he's our enemy. We thought that God was good, but in our inexplicable suffering, we start to wonder if he's a monster. We know what the Bible says, but our circumstances cause us to waver and stumble. Is God really for us, or has he turned against us?

Completely Answering Versus Competently Addressing

Diving into the deep end of suffering and trying to wrap our minds around the truths that we need to keep afloat is a difficult task. On one hand, it would be wrong to think that we can fully access the mind and will of God in such a way that all our questions are answered to the degree that we desire. We should be wary when people think that they can tell us exactly what God is up to in our comprehensive and chronic suffering. Yet it would also be wrong to just throw up our hands and say that we can't truly know anything about God's ways, will, promises, and plans. This way of thinking deprives us of the truths that can stabilize and strengthen us to keep moving forward.

Complete answers and complete avoidance are both erroneous approaches that fail to strengthen sufferers with truth, grace, and hope. But there is a third way. While we can never *completely answer* these hard questions and should never *completely avoid* them, we can seek to *competently address* them according to what God has revealed to us in his Word. It is a weighty thing to accurately convey the truth about who God is, especially when it comes to suffering. And while God doesn't choose to completely answer the questions of his children, may what appears in the following pages help rekindle faith and hope in the hearts of weary sufferers wondering who God is in light of their affliction.

Bewildered Saints

Counter to the false teaching of the prosperity gospel, Scripture pulls no punches concerning the painful internal and external experiences that believers will face in a fallen world, including our experience of our relationship with God. Listen to how suffering believers speak to and about God in Scripture:

> What is man, that you [God] make so much of him,
>> and that you set your heart on him,
> visit him every morning
>> and test him every moment?
> How long will you not look away from me,
>> nor leave me alone till I swallow my spit?
> If I sin, what do I do to you, you watcher of mankind?
>> *Why have you made me your mark?* (Job 7:17–20)

> If I summoned [God] and he answered me,
>> I would not believe that he was listening to my voice.
> For he crushes me with a tempest
>> and *multiplies my wounds without cause.* (Job 9:16–17)

When disaster brings sudden death,
    [God] mocks at the calamity of the innocent.
The earth is given into the hand of the wicked;
    he covers the faces of its judges—
    if it is not he, who then is it? (Job 9:23–24)

I was at ease, and *[God] broke me apart*;
    he seized me by the neck and dashed me to pieces;
he set me up as his target;
    his archers surround me.
He slashes open my kidneys and does not spare;
    he pours out my gall on the ground.
He breaks me with breach upon breach;
    he runs upon me like a warrior. (Job 16:12–14)

My face is red with weeping,
    and on my eyelids is deep darkness,
although there is no violence in my hands,
    and my prayer is pure. (Job 16:16–17)

[God] has walled up my way, so that I cannot pass,
    and he has set darkness upon my paths.
He has stripped from me my glory
    and taken the crown from my head.
He breaks me down on every side, and I am gone,
    and my hope has he pulled up like a tree. (Job 19:8–10)

For [God] will complete what he appoints for me,
    and many such things are in his mind.
Therefore *I am terrified at his presence*;
    when I consider, I am in dread of him.

God has made my heart faint;
    the Almighty has terrified me. (Job 23:14–16)

God has cast me into the mire,
    and I have become like dust and ashes.
I cry to you for help and you do not answer me;
    I stand, and you only look at me.
You have turned cruel to me;
    with the might of your hand you persecute me.
You lift me up on the wind; you make me ride on it,
    and you toss me about in the roar of the storm. (Job
        30:19–22)

When I hoped for good, evil came,
    and when I waited for light, darkness came. (Job 30:26)

I am the man who has seen affliction
    under the rod of [God's] wrath;
he has driven and brought me
    into darkness without any light;
surely against me he turns his hand
    again and again the whole day long. (Lam. 3:1–3)

[God] has besieged and enveloped me
    with bitterness and tribulation;
he has made me dwell in darkness
    like the dead of long ago.
He has walled me about so that I cannot escape;
    he has made my chains heavy;
though I call and cry for help,
    he shuts out my prayer;

> he has blocked my ways with blocks of stones;
>> he has made my paths crooked. (Lam. 3:5–9)

> *[God] has made my teeth grind on gravel,*
>> *and made me cower in ashes;*
> my soul is bereft of peace;
>> I have forgotten what happiness is;
> so I say, "My endurance has perished;
>> so has my hope from the LORD." (Lam. 3:16–18)

These are words that only those who have known deep darkness can relate to. We can sense their crushing weight, bewildered terror, sinking despair, and dark conclusions. Yet these are not the words of the arrogant atheist or the immature Christian. These are the words of some of Scripture's most righteous men: God's servant Job and the prophet Jeremiah.

Comprehensive and chronic suffering can rattle the core of what believers treasure most: our relationship with the Lord. We may wonder, Does God care about what's happening to me? Is he angry with me? Why is he allowing me to experience such unrelenting and life-draining affliction? In other words, profound suffering can bring godly believers to a crisis of faith that they never would have imagined possible in brighter days. Suffering can blast apart the life narrative and interpretational grid that we've spent years developing, shattering them into a million tiny pieces. Life no longer makes sense; the pieces that once fit together no longer fit. You thought you knew who God was. You thought you knew how he operated. You thought you knew which end was up and which end was down. But now, nothing you thought you knew matches with your current experience. And despite all your biblical and theological knowledge, such suffering can make you feel as though you're back to square one in your understanding of God.

For reasons that we are not privy to, God does not bring all his children to this place. Not all believers experience a depth of affliction that shakes their faith and worldview to the core. Those who don't experience severe suffering may be tempted to judge those who do, perhaps even believing that if they experienced such overwhelming suffering, they would sail through their affliction on a cloud of triumphant glory.

That is one reason why it's so critical for us to keep coming back to the Scriptures, where God shows us what can happen when human beings are crushed by deep affliction. Despite how some misguided believers might respond to those who utter sentiments like the ones found in the books of Job, Lamentations, and Psalms, God is the one who preserved those words as part of the canon of Scripture. Their inclusion "shows us that we are not alone in our doubts, confusions, and complaints. Not only have other believers felt the same things, but God has inscripturated those sentiments to assure us that it is legitimate to feel such things and to pour them out in prayer."[2]

The God Who Invites Us to Speak

When we look more closely at the words of Job, Jeremiah, and the psalmists, we realize that they communicate a precious truth about who God is and what he is like. Imagine for a moment that you were to speak some of the words quoted above during a time of sharing in your church small group. How do you think that would go? Spiritually mature group members would likely respond appropriately. But it might make those who are less mature uncomfortable at best and combative at worst.

But God himself made sure that these laments and hard words were included in Scripture. He didn't have to do that. He could have cut them out like a master editor, ensuring that only the words that sounded full of joy, gratitude, and faith made it into the final draft of the Bible.

Do you see how good, kind, merciful, and patient God is? God himself gives us scripts to model our response to pain after. He shows us that such feelings, thoughts, and words should be expressed to him. He *wants* us to come *to* him with our confusion *about* him. And so, even as we struggle in our relationship with God, the fact that God himself acknowledges this struggle and gives us divinely inspired words to use in that struggle shows us something good about God's heart toward us.

How We Feel Versus What Is True

It's also important to clarify that many of these hard words from Job, Jeremiah, and the psalmists are inaccurate in a strictly doctrinal sense. They're not true affirmations of God's character and attributes, nor are they intended to be. Rather, these people are describing how they are feeling amid their deep turmoil and what they are thinking amid their swirling confusion.

For example, statements about God's absence cannot be actual statements of fact, since God is present everywhere in his creation (see Ps. 139). But here, the writers are being honest about their experience, about their feeling as if God were absent even though, properly speaking, he cannot be. God invites such words despite their theological inaccuracy, however, because they help us pour out our confusion and despair to him rather than trying to repress them or process them on our own.

So, let's remember to hold both together: God wants us to speak honest words to him, and doing so helps unburden our hearts. But we should also remember that some of our words may be untrue. And God is gracious to us as we seek to rebuild from the ashes a biblical worldview that creates space for both a good and loving God and comprehensive and chronic suffering.

God's Heart

Does God care about me? Why does it seem like he's being cruel to me? Where is his compassion for me? Perhaps these questions, more than any other, plague people in their relationship with God when they are experiencing comprehensive and chronic suffering. We've seen Job and Jeremiah wrestle with thoughts like these. Job uttered the following words about God: "[He] multiplies my wounds without cause. . . . He mocks at the calamity of the innocent" (Job 9:17, 23). Jeremiah says, "[God] has made my teeth grind on gravel" (Lam. 3:16). Causing someone pain for no good reason, mocking at the suffering of the innocent, and pushing another person's face into the ground is cruel, not caring.

Job and Jeremiah felt this way about God at various points in their suffering. But is this really who God is and what he is like? The book of Lamentations helps us answer this question. While Lamentations 3:22–23 is often emphasized in sermons and messages as the high point of the book—"The steadfast love of the Lord never ceases; his mercies never come to an end; they are new every morning; great is your faithfulness"—the center verse from a structural standpoint is actually Lamentations 3:33. This verse lies at the *exact* middle point not only of chapter 3 but of the entire book, and it helps answer a question faced by sufferers that even verses 22–23 do not. What hope is there for those with dark thoughts about God? Scripture says, "[God] does not afflict from his heart or grieve the children of men" (Lam. 3:33).

Before we delve into why this is such good news for sufferers, it's important to make sure that we understand the context of the book of Lamentations. Scholars usually attribute some or all of this book to Jeremiah, though we can't know this with certainty, since no author is mentioned. The book's laments are a response to the destruction of Judah and Jerusalem at the hands of the Babylonians, who served as God's vehicle of judgment for his corrupt and unrepentant people. Of course, not everyone in Judah was wicked and unrepentant at the time this judgment took place. Jeremiah himself was a godly man who suffered the impact of God's judgment on Judah's wickedness. Yet this truth in Lamentations 3:33 is good news for sufferers in two ways.

First, it tells us point-blank who God is and who God isn't. He is not an uncaring or cruel God who delights in the suffering of his people. And second, since this book is written in the context of sin and judgment, it shows us that if God does not afflict from his heart even in the context of his people's blatant wickedness and rebellion, then he certainly doesn't afflict from his heart those who, like Job, have sought to honor and serve him yet find themselves being called to walk the path of comprehensive and chronic suffering.

Isaiah 63:9 also tells us something about God's heart for his suffering people: "In all their affliction [God] was afflicted." This means that God identifies with his people to such an extent that "he takes what injury is done to them as done to himself and will reckon for it accordingly. Their cries move him (Ex. 3:7), and he appears for them as vigorously as if he were pained in their pain."[3]

How are we then to understand the horrible affliction that comes our way when we believe in a God who is both sovereign and good? Christopher Ash notes, "When God acts in steadfast love and faithfulness, these actions express his character directly. But when evil things happen, God is acting through the agencies of evil powers, and the actions do not reveal his character. They are part of his grand plan to turn evil to good, to defeat evil, but they do not immediately reveal his character."[4] As we saw in chapter 3, these evil things reveal the heart of Satan, not the heart of God.

Ash further states, "The hands and fingers that destroyed Job's possessions and killed Job's children and wrecked Job's health were the hands of the Satan, not the hands of God. Yes, it was the hand of the Satan acting with the permission of the Lord and within the strict constraints given by the Lord; but it was the Satan's hand and not God's that actually did these terrible things."[5]

We've seen from Lamentations 3 that God is not cruel in our suffering. But does he really care? If Scripture makes clear that God doesn't delight in our suffering, does it also tell us that God really does care for us, even when he calls us to walk through comprehensive and chronic suffering? Psalm 56:8 says this: "You have kept count of my tossings; put my tears in your bottle. Are they not in your book?" Commenting on this verse, Matthew Henry says that God observes his people "with compassion and tender concern; he is afflicted in their afflictions, and knows their souls in adversity. As the blood of his saints, and their deaths, are precious in the sight of the Lord, so are their tears, not one of them shall fall to the ground. . . . What was sown a tear will come up a pearl."[6]

No one in their right mind saves things they find worthless. We save things that we value, whether that value is material or sentimental. So, if God is keeping track of our tossings, if he puts our tears in his bottle, then surely he cares deeply about us, our suffering, and our pain.

We learn something more about our tears in Revelation 21:4, which says, "[God] will wipe away every tear from their eyes." It's hard to conceive of anything more tender or caring than one person holding up their hand to another person's face and gently wiping their wet, tear-stained cheeks. This is reserved for only the most intimate of relationships: parent to child, spouse to spouse, best friend to best friend. And God chose this word picture to reveal the depths of his care for us and the closeness of the relationship we have with him. Note that God doesn't send a proxy to wipe our tears away first before we approach him. He doesn't give us a moment to go to a celestial restroom and collect ourselves before we meet him. Rather, he is intimately and personally involved. He wants to be the one who wipes the tears away.

This text also reveals a truth that may help us with the seeming incongruity between our affliction and God's love. In the imagery of the book of Revelation, the saints show up to heaven crying. In other words, God's love and care for them has not precluded them from experiencing sorrow and affliction until their last day on earth. They're still weeping when they get to heaven. Paradoxically, the same God who wipes their tears away is the one who ordained their tears in the first place. The fact of our weeping and affliction on earth doesn't mean that God has forsaken us—but perhaps it does mean that our joy will be all the greater when one day he spends the time to wipe away those tears for good.

Without a doubt, it can be very difficult for us to see God as compassionate when he ordains that we experience deep affliction. We read verses such as Psalm 103:13–14, which say,

> As a father shows compassion to his children,
>> so the LORD shows compassion to those who fear him.
> For he knows our frame;
>> he remembers that we are dust.

Yet when we look at the comprehensive and chronic suffering that our sovereign God has ordained for us, we can begin to think, "A good earthly father would never allow his child to experience this kind of affliction if he had the power to stop it. And if earthly fathers are just a pale reflection of God, the ultimately good Father, what does that say about God? Do earthly parents (or, for that matter, anyone who sees another person facing affliction and wishes they had the power to change it) have more compassion for humans than God does, since he does have the power to protect us from such deep suffering but chooses not to?"

This is a hard question to answer. I'm not even sure if there is an "answer" that will completely satisfy us in this life (which we'll talk about more in the section on God's holiness). But one thing to consider regarding this tough question is this: Ultimately, God's compassion toward us must be defined and understood in light of our future eternal state in the new heavens and new earth. What does this mean? It means that, sometimes, what might not look like compassion from a narrower frame of reference actually proves to be compassion from a wider frame of reference.

Imagine watching a movie that opens with a close-up scene of a mother and father with their sleepy young child. We see them shaking the child and screaming at her. Understandably, we conclude that the child is a victim of abusive parents and that she needs to be rescued from them. But then, the camera lens widens, and we see more of what is happening. From the broader vantage point, we now see that the family is trapped in a howling snowstorm, and the parents are desperately trying to prevent their beloved child from succumbing to hypothermia. We draw a completely different—in fact, opposite—conclusion from the exact same circumstance, now that we've been given the benefit of the whole picture.

This means that, from our temporal and limited vantage point, it will sometimes appear as though God lacks compassion for us and is even being cruel or malicious toward us. But if we believe that we can't see the complete picture of all that he is doing, it means that God's treatment of us now in our earthly lives will prove to have been filled with compassion once we have the vantage point of eternity (see James 5:11). God has that vantage point now. We, as finite and limited human beings, do not. And though it's not easy, we are called to walk by faith until the day our faith becomes sight and we understand why God has dealt with us the way that he has. God never told Job what we know about why he allowed Job's sufferings. Job had to trust him with that unanswered question. But God did reveal enough of himself to Job to make walking by faith a reasonable request, and he's revealed enough of himself through the cross of Jesus Christ to make it possible for us to do that too.

God's Silence and Absence

"Why doesn't God answer any of my prayers? And why don't I sense his presence at all in my suffering?" These, too, are deeply painful and perplexing questions for many people who experience comprehensive and chronic suffering. They become especially hard when contrasted with testimonies of other Christians who have had a very different experience of suffering. We hear stories of how, in their deepest affliction, God amazingly and clearly answered their prayers. Or we hear about how, in their deepest tragedy, they experienced God's presence, care, and love in more powerful ways than they'd ever known.

This is more than simply confusing to Christians who don't have the same experience; it can be terrifying. Why? Because if others have experienced God's nearness, and if our experience is that of his silence and absence, then we assume either that we must be doing something horribly wrong or that we are self-deceived and do not even belong to God in the first place. The question is, Does Scripture confirm that we can be God's beloved children yet experience his silence and absence in our affliction?

This is the real question behind our questions about God's silence and absence. We can begin to see him as apathetic and uncaring, or even angry and hostile, toward us. That's why we're looking at so many scriptural examples in this book. When we fear that we must be outside the circle of God's favor, stories of saints with similar experiences remind us that we can encounter difficult circumstances, and even turmoil and doubt in our relationship with God, yet still be safe and secure in the circle of his love, care, and salvation.

Both Job and Jeremiah testify to a sense of God's silence and absence:

> I cry to you for help and you do not answer me;
> > I stand, and you only look at me.
> You have turned cruel to me;
> > with the might of your hand you persecute me. (Job
> > > 30:20–21)

> Though I call and cry for help,
> > he shuts out my prayer;
> he has blocked my ways with blocks of stones;
> > he has made my paths crooked. (Lam. 3:8–9)

Both men experienced unanswered prayers and a deep sense of God's absence rather than his loving care. Worse still, any "presence" of God that either one felt was the presence of cruelty and antagonism, not care and attention.

But Job and Jeremiah aren't the only ones who felt God's silence and absence in their affliction. Consider this psalm written by Heman the Ezrahite, one of the Sons of Korah. It is worth quoting in its entirety:

> O Lord, God of my salvation,
> > I cry out day and night before you.
> Let my prayer come before you;
> > incline your ear to my cry!

For my soul is full of troubles,
    and my life draws near to Sheol.
I am counted among those who go down to the pit;
    I am a man who has no strength,
like one set loose among the dead,
    like the slain that lie in the grave,
like those whom you remember no more,
    for they are cut off from your hand.
You have put me in the depths of the pit,
    in the regions dark and deep.
Your wrath lies heavy upon me,
    and you overwhelm me with all your waves.

You have caused my companions to shun me;
    you have made me a horror to them.
I am shut in so that I cannot escape;
    my eye grows dim through sorrow.
Every day I call upon you, O Lord;
    I spread out my hands to you.
Do you work wonders for the dead?
    Do the departed rise up to praise you?
Is your steadfast love declared in the grave,
    or your faithfulness in Abaddon?
Are your wonders known in the darkness,
    or your righteousness in the land of forgetfulness?

But I, O Lord, cry to you;
    in the morning my prayer comes before you.
O Lord, why do you cast my soul away?
    Why do you hide your face from me?
Afflicted and close to death from my youth up,

I suffer your terrors; I am helpless.
Your wrath has swept over me;
 your dreadful assaults destroy me.
They surround me like a flood all day long;
 they close in on me together.
You have caused my beloved and my friend to shun me;
 my companions have become darkness. (Ps. 88:1–18)

This is the only psalm in the Psalter that does not end on a note of faith or hope. Instead, it ends with darkness. Was this a mistake? Should this psalm have not been included in God's inspired and inerrant Word? Of course, we know that what appears in the Bible is what God wants to be there, so he indeed has a purpose for including Psalm 88 in the canon of Scripture. While some may look at this psalm and consider it hopeless, it can actually provide great hope for people experiencing difficulty and disorientation in their relationship with God in their suffering. It shows us that our experience of deep darkness need not indicate that we do not belong to the Lord, and it shows us that this darkness can persist longer than we'd like.

Scripture is filled with examples of what seem like excessive delays on God's part. Early in the pages of Genesis, we see Noah's parents hoping that their son would be the one to fulfill the promise of the seed who would crush the serpent's head (see Gen. 5:28–29). Yet what Noah's parents hoped for was still thousands of years away. The people of Israel suffered as slaves in Egypt for hundreds of years before God delivered them. Joseph waited for years to be rescued from prison and restored to his family. Heman was still waiting at the time of his song in Psalm 88 for God to answer his prayer. The woman with the issue of blood and the man born blind, whom we meet

in the Gospels, likely prayed for years before they received healing from the only one who can help make sense of our stories
of suffering and waiting: the Promised One, the Messiah, the
serpent-crusher, the sin-bearer, the suffering Savior whose
suffering guarantees that our suffering will one day end.

He is the one who knows what it's like to wait and to suffer.
When Jesus was on the cross, the crowd said, "He trusts in
God; let God deliver him now, if he desires him. For he said, 'I
am the Son of God'" (Matt. 27:43). Yet what the crowds didn't
understand was that if the Father rescued Jesus from the cross
and ended his suffering right then and there, the suffering of
every human being who has ever lived and will ever live would
never have ended, for there would have been no righteous
Redeemer to pay the penalty for our sins and impart to us a
righteousness that we have not earned and could not earn.

God's delays in our lives and in the lives of our loved ones
rarely make sense to us. But when we look at Scripture, we
gain a broader vantage point as we see God's good purposes
in the lives of people who suffered and waited. Therefore,
let's believe that the same God who brought good from their
suffering and waiting will do so for us as well, even if we can't
see it in this life. Just because we have experienced a sense of
God's silence and absence doesn't mean that we don't belong
to him, that he doesn't care, that he's not listening, or that
he's not there.

The Incomprehensibility of God

We've already noted in this chapter that some of God's
ways are inaccessible and inscrutable to us. Theologians refer
to this as God's *incomprehensibility*. This doesn't mean that

we can't comprehend God at all but rather that humans cannot comprehend him exhaustively. The finite cannot fully grasp the infinite. For his own purposes, God does not allow us to see the whole picture. We may find that fact unpalatable or disturbing, but the truth is that it would be much more disturbing if that weren't the case. It would be disturbing if our own intelligence were so on par with God's that frail, finite, sinful, time-bound human beings could expect to access and understand divine knowledge in the same way he does.

That is why, as we seek to draw near to God through Scripture and understand who he is and isn't, we must also understand our limitations. We must recognize that even though it's true that we are created in his image, there is a big difference between the Creator and the creature. Romans 11:33 says, "Oh, the depth of the riches and wisdom and knowledge of God! How unsearchable are his judgments and how inscrutable his ways!" If we could fully plumb the depths of God's wisdom and knowledge, if we could easily search out his judgments and make clear sense of all his ways, what would that say about God? It would only say that he's really not that much different from us.

Often, when we consider God's holiness, the first definition that comes to mind is that of moral purity and perfection. And that's certainly accurate. But God's holiness also has another meaning, namely, that he is "separate" from his creation in a unique way; he is "other" than his creatures. In other words, he is in a category all his own. So, while we can expect him to reveal many things to us that we can understand (which he has), we must at the same time acknowledge that God's holy incomprehensibility means that sometimes (or even often) we won't understand his ways to the degree that we'd like to. Yet what we *do* know about God is enough for us to trust him for what we *don't* know about him. And what's clear about God is enough for us to trust him for what we find confusing about him.

From Adversary to Advocate

As we've noted already, though Job's external circumstances were indeed excruciating, his deepest pain in all his affliction was the change he perceived in his relationship with God. The God who had always been *for* him now appeared to be ferociously *against* him. Job had no way to account for this change, since he walked in uprightness and integrity. And his miserable comforters only reinforced the idea that God was indeed angry at him and that his sin must be the reason for this state of affairs.

Many sufferers have turned to the book of Job in their affliction and been partly helped and partly confused by it. On one hand, its portrayal of innocent suffering and Job's honest speeches can comfort sufferers who feel kinship with Job's external circumstances and internal anguish. But for modern readers, God's speeches at the end of the book can leave us scratching our heads and a bit disappointed. I read God's speeches many times in my own suffering and wondered what I was missing. I couldn't see a link between what God said to Job and the profound joy and peace that Job experienced as a result of these interactions. To be honest, I felt somewhat stupid and spiritually defective—why weren't these speeches helping me as much as they helped Job?

To make matters worse, I had listened to sermons and read books on Job that seemed to indicate that God's speeches to Job were meant merely to communicate his absolute sovereignty and raw power, so that Job would simply sit down and shut up. But Job was already aware of God's raw power and sovereignty—so much so that he grew terrified of God. It doesn't make sense, then, that the message "I'm bigger and more powerful than you, Job, so shut up and trust me" would in any way comfort Job at the book's end.

But we begin to see why God's speeches are so helpful to Job when we understand the symbolism behind some of the references within them. In Job 40–41, God speaks of "Behemoth" and "Leviathan." While these references may be describing animals such as the hippopotamus and the crocodile, on a symbolic level, they represent the dark and sinister spiritual forces of evil—forces that "God can control but before which Job is helpless."[7]

This would have comforted Job on multiple levels. First, it reoriented his understanding of who the true enemy was. He realized that God did not consider him an enemy. Rather, Leviathan (Satan) was the one inflicting misery upon him in an attempt to detract from God's glory and destroy Job's faith. Second, Job gained courage and hope from God's superior power to defeat the enemy: "Satan and his forces of evil have no more power than God allows them. He is able to treat them like tame household pets."[8]

Everything changed when Job realized that God was not his adversary but was, in fact, his advocate. In Job 38–41, "God reveals Himself as Job's friend, bringing him before the astonishing works of creation to show him that the One he has reproached is sovereign in goodness and power. Job recognizes that God is and remains his friend."[9] Though he had spoken "words without knowledge" in his suffering (of which he repented before the Lord), God expanded Job's understanding of him such that his disorientation and despair gave way to awe, relief, adoration, and hope.

It is easy to look at someone else's story from an objective point of view and retain a true perspective on God's character. It is usually easy to look at small or fleeting suffering in our own lives and retain that same perspective. But as we have noted, comprehensive and chronic suffering that resembles Job's experience is something quite different. A defining feature of this struggle is the force with which it assaults our perception and experience of who God is, who we are, and how we relate to him.

Because the nature of this struggle involves laboring to understand who God is and how that relates to our circumstances in deeper ways, it is rarely helpful to sufferers when people simply quote Bible verses at them and expect that to instantly fix the "problem." Our triune God is thoroughly relational, and being a Christian is relational at its core. Relationship is so foundational that Jesus says that he will tell some people to depart from him, despite their outward ministry, because "I never knew you" (Matt. 7:23). Therefore, our greatest struggle in comprehensive and chronic suffering is to persevere as we continue speaking to the God who feels so absent, so hostile, so different from who we once experienced him as. It is a process of walking by faith as we refuse to curse God or give up.

Job waited for a long time before the Lord, in his own timing, appeared to him. God will "appear" to us as well through his Word, his Spirit, and his people, gradually but surely restoring our relationship to him by bringing us into a deeper and more mature understanding of himself. He will reach each of us in unique ways to reaffirm his character, and as a result, we will experience comfort in him once again. This may not happen in such a "big" moment as it did for Job, but God promises us that "none who wait for [him] shall be put to shame" (Ps. 25:3).

God's Son: The Suffering God-Man

Believers today enjoy a much greater knowledge and understanding of God than Job did. Job was a devout worshiper of God, but he lived during a period in redemptive history when so much was unclear and unknown. The events in the book of Job occurred in a non-Israelite setting, and although we don't know this with certainty, he likely lived during the patriarchal period. Job knew nothing of God's redemption of his people from slavery in Egypt, or of their conquest of the promised land, or of the splendor of David's and Solomon's kingdoms, or of the Old Testament prophecies that were fulfilled. And he didn't have the full knowledge of the one whom his life foreshadowed—the only truly righteous sufferer, our Lord Jesus Christ.

Can you imagine going through comprehensive and chronic suffering before the life, death, and resurrection of Christ? Comparing Job's suffering to the suffering of Jesus, Christopher Ash comments, "[Jesus] knew a real God-forsakenness at the same time he was the Father's beloved Son. This feeling of God-forsakenness is also an authentic part of Christian experience. It is possible to be—objectively—a dearly beloved son or daughter of God while also experiencing—subjectively and in part—all the ingredients of Job's experience here."[10]

It is Jesus, God who took on flesh, who most clearly reveals God to us, helping reorient the skewed view of God that deep affliction and Satan's temptations can create. Reflecting on Athanasius's writings on the incarnation of Christ, Kelly Kapic observes,

> Since sin affected us holistically, it not only corrupted our bodies, bringing physical pain and death, but it also corrupted our vision of God himself. Fallen humanity was left to imagine God as cruel and unconcerned. This again gets to the hard thoughts about God we might be tempted to have. Jesus, the Word of God incarnate, replaces the distorted picture of God that we have with an accurate portrait of the Father of the Lord Jesus Christ. . . . We have a chance, through the incarnation, to have a restored vision of the God who is, rather than a distorted image of a god we fear. . . . Put simply, to see Jesus is to see the Father, for he comes from the Father and reveals the Father full of grace and truth.[11]

Despite the forsakenness or hostility we may perceive in our affliction, we have the assurance on this side of the cross that "God shows his love for us in that while we were still sinners, Christ died for us" (Rom. 5:8). And though "we are being killed all the day long" and "regarded as sheep to be slaughtered," we are promised that nothing "will be able to separate us from the love of God in Christ Jesus our Lord" (Rom. 8:36, 39). God may permit and ordain unspeakable suffering in our lives. But as we have seen, the hostility and malice come from Satan, and the good purposes come from God: "Behold, we consider those blessed who remained steadfast. You have heard of the steadfastness of Job, and you have seen the purpose of the Lord, how the Lord is compassionate and merciful" (James 5:11).

Part 2

Comprehensive and Chronic Suffering

5

HOW GOD TREATS
HIS FRIENDS

When we suffer, it can be hard to look around at the blessings that some Christians enjoy and wonder what happened with our lives. Social media does not help, as it gives us front-row seats to the blessings of hundreds of people we know (and millions of people we don't know). While even the average person in relatively pleasant circumstances can struggle in this way, the experience is greatly compounded for those enduring comprehensive suffering precisely because of its comprehensiveness.

It's one thing to envy the prosperity of the wicked. Asaph describes his own experience of that in Psalm 73, and this psalm is instructive for believers who envy the blessings of unbelievers. But how are Christians who experience comprehensive suffering to understand their lives in contrast to the more prosperous *believers* around them who seem to suffer much less? Why does God treat his children so differently?

Does he play favorites? Why is there so much apparent inequity of circumstances among believers, and how are we to understand that disparity?

These questions can plague those experiencing comprehensive suffering. Not only can these disparities tempt us to disbelieve God's goodness, but they can also lead us to doubt our standing before God. We might conclude that if God is taking his other children on a field trip and we're left behind at school to stand in the corner all day—or, even worse, thrown under the school bus—we must have done something to anger him. Hard thoughts about God, other Christians, and ourselves can overwhelm us as we get pulled into the undertow of our observations and conclusions.

The question we must answer is this: How does God treat his friends?

One of These Things Is Not Like the Other

For many of us who live in the West, it can be hard to gain an accurate perspective of the Christian life. Our moment is quite abnormal compared to other parts of the world and other eras in history. And when the abnormal becomes normal to us, any deviation from that norm makes us feel as though something has gone awry.

In this milieu, it can be easy for us to look at the comfortable lives of the average Christians around us and conclude that something has gone horribly wrong for us. This is especially the case when our suffering is comprehensive, touching many areas of our lives at the same time: our physical health, our finances, our church involvement, our friendships, our careers, our families, and our homes and belongings. When this occurs, our daily lives and rhythms become so different from those of most of the people we know that we can feel as though we don't belong. When it seems as though others are prospering in these various areas of life while we are experiencing deep loss and affliction in most (or all) of them, we may wonder, Why does God seem to be treating me so differently from his other children? Is this a sign that I don't belong to him?

That's what's so hard about comprehensive suffering: Because it invades more parts of life than it leaves alone, it places you in a strange new world in which you may struggle to relate to the average Christian in your church. You may become very aware of the fact that what is "normal life" for many of the Christians around you is nothing like your life. It might even become difficult to have casual conversations with other believers. Maybe you feel like a deer caught in the headlights when you're asked about "normal" things that don't apply to you at all and you can't give the answers that people expect.

When that happens, the place where we should feel like we belong the most—in the church and among fellow believers—can become the place where we feel most different, most "other," most out of place. It's hard to put into words how draining and discouraging these experiences in the house of God are. How do we answer people's questions or contribute to the group conversation when everyone else's lives and concerns are so different from ours and we cannot relate to them in these ways?

It's not surprising, therefore, that those experiencing comprehensive suffering can be tempted to conclude that God is cruel or unkind in how he dispenses temporal blessings to his children. It's not surprising if sufferers fear that they must be guilty of some sin, that if they could only figure it out, God would take them out of the corner and let them go on the field trip too. It's also easy to see how sufferers can feel that they simply don't belong at church, when conversations always seem to revolve around the differences between their lives and others' lives rather than around that which they hold in common.

All this is why we must turn to Scripture to try to make sense of the painful question of inequity among believers in this life, allowing God's Word to shape our interpretations of our experiences rather than the other way around.

What Scripture Says

What does Scripture say about how God treats his friends? More than we might expect. In fact, when we look closely at redemptive history, we see that it was often the people used by God in mighty ways who led what we would consider the "worst" lives. That fact in itself can encourage us if we're tempted to believe that we must not be friends of God if we're experiencing comprehensive suffering. After all, many whom we might consider to be God's "closest friends" suffered in profound ways during their earthly lives. In this section, we'll take a brief look at some of these friends of God.

Bereft Job

We talk a lot about Job throughout this book, and for good reason. He is a prime example of a righteous believer who was loved by God yet experienced inexplicable suffering. He "feared God and turned away from evil" (Job 1:1). He took great care to worship God well. After his children's feasts had concluded, "Job would send and consecrate them, and he would rise early in the morning and offer burnt offerings according to the number of them all. For Job said, 'It may be that my children have sinned, and cursed God in their hearts.' Thus Job did continually" (v. 5).

God himself praises Job before Satan: "Have you considered my servant Job, that there is none like him on the earth, a blameless and upright man, who fears God and turns away from evil?" (v. 8). Job was devoted to the Lord, and this is abundantly clear in how God himself speaks of Job. He said that one godlier than Job could not be found.

Yet despite (and actually because of) Job's righteousness and God's love for him, God allows Satan to destroy Job's animals, servants, children, and health. And except for a chapter at the beginning and a few chapters at the end, most of the book chronicles painful dialogues between Job and his foolish friends as he is overwhelmed with comprehensive suffering and struggles to make sense of his relationship with God in light of his circumstances and his understanding of how the world worked.

God reaffirms his commendation of Job at the close of the book, saying, "My anger burns against you [Eliphaz] and against your two friends, for you have not spoken of me what is right, as my servant Job has" (42:7). In fact, Job serves as a mediator between his miserable comforters and God: "My servant Job shall pray for you, for I will accept his prayer not to deal with you according to your folly. For you have not spoken of me what is right, as my servant Job has" (v. 8).

Job was dearly loved by God and a faithful servant of God. He was a friend of God. Yet God permitted (and actually instigated) the painful events in Job's life, with the result that

Job beheld God in a new and deeper way, God's honor was upheld, Job's friends had the opportunity to repent of their foolishness and grow in true wisdom, and Job's future became even more glorious than his life before his suffering had been. While our earthly stories may not end with prosperity like Job's did, his is ultimately a picture of our eternal inheritance in the new heavens and new earth, where God will honor his faithful servants and friends who endure suffering.

Weeping Jeremiah

Jeremiah is sometimes known as "the weeping prophet," and it's not difficult to see why. His calling led to much loneliness (see Jer. 15:17). The Lord did not permit him to marry or have children (see Jer. 16:1–2). His own people wanted to put him to death for the prophecies he made against Israel (see Jer. 26:8). Perhaps contrary to what we might expect from a prophet of the Lord, "[Jeremiah] expresses his anguish at the great burden of his prophetic calling, prays for vengeance on his personal enemies, and even accuses the Lord of having forced or deceived him (15:18; 20:7)."[1]

In addition to these difficulties, "his messages of repentance delivered at the temple were not well received (7:1–8:3; 26:1–11). His hometown plotted against him (11:18–23), and he endured much persecution in the pursuit of his ministry (20:1–6; 37:11–38:13; 43:1–7). . . . Though the book does not reveal the time or place of Jeremiah's death, he presumably died in Egypt, where he had been taken by his countrymen against his will after the fall of Jerusalem (43:1–7)."[2] Chosen by God, this friend of God lived what we would consider an "abnormal" life and faithfully walked a lonely road despite a seemingly pointless ministry, all before dying in a foreign land.

Imprisoned John

John the Baptist had miraculous beginnings. He was born to barren and elderly parents. He was filled with the Holy Spirit from his mother's womb (see Luke 1:15) and became a prophet. Many Israelites came to be baptized by him and followed him (see Matt. 3:5–6). Our Lord Jesus even noted, "Truly, I say to you, among those born of women there has arisen no one greater than John the Baptist" (Matt. 11:11). But let's see what happened to this beloved friend of God.

John confronted the ruler Herod, telling him that it was unlawful for him to take his brother's wife as his own. Unsurprisingly, this angered Herod, and he threw John in prison (see Matt. 14:3–4). While in prison, John heard about the works being done by Jesus, so he had his disciples send this message to Jesus: "Are you the one who is to come, or shall we look for another?" (Matt. 11:3).

What led John the Baptist to ask such a question? Didn't he already know that Jesus was the Messiah? "John is probably concerned because his present imprisonment does not match his understanding of the Coming One's arrival, which was to bring blessing on those who repented and judgment on those who did not."[3] In other words, John's expectations for what would happen when the Messiah came were not coming to fruition. In fact, the opposite appeared to be happening. "Presumably John heard reports of Jesus' exorcisms and miraculous healings, which show that He is the Messiah. But Jesus allows His forerunner to be imprisoned by the wicked

Herod, evoking John's question whether He is indeed the royal executor of divine justice for which God's suffering people have been longing."[4]

We can relate to John's perplexity as we compare our expectations for our lives as God's people with the reality of our comprehensive suffering. Yet this is often the way for the friends of God: Suffering precedes glory.

What became of the forerunner of the Messiah? At Herod's birthday party, the daughter of Herodias "danced before the company and pleased Herod" (Matt. 14:6). This led Herod to offer her anything she wished, and, at her mother's prompting, she asked for the head of John the Baptist on a platter. This beloved friend of God spent his last days in a prison cell before being beheaded.

Abandoned Paul

In chapter 2, we noted the suffering that the apostle Paul faced at the hands of friends and ministry partners who abandoned him. Yet Paul suffered in many other ways as a friend of God. As a sampling of some of these sufferings, Paul tells the Corinthians,

> Are they servants of Christ? I am a better one—I am talking like a madman—with far greater labors, far more imprisonments, with countless beatings, and often near death. Five times I received at the hands of the Jews the forty lashes less one. Three times I was beaten with rods. Once I was stoned. Three times I was shipwrecked; a night and a day I was adrift at sea; on frequent journeys, in danger from rivers, danger from robbers, danger from my own people, danger from Gentiles, danger in the city, danger in the wilderness, danger at

sea, danger from false brothers; in toil and hardship, through many a sleepless night, in hunger and thirst, often without food, in cold and exposure. And, apart from other things, there is the daily pressure on me of my anxiety for all the churches. Who is weak, and I am not weak? Who is made to fall, and I am not indignant? (2 Cor. 11:23–29)

Not only that, but in order that Paul would remain humble despite the greatness of the revelations he received from the Lord, he was afflicted with "a thorn . . . in the flesh, a messenger of Satan to harass [him]" (2 Cor. 12:7). Despite praying to the Lord three times that this thorn would be removed, Paul received no relief (see vv. 8–9). Since Paul nowhere states the nature of this thorn, we don't know for certain what it was. Commentators have speculated that it could have been a physical affliction, demonic harassment, human enemies, or something else. But whatever it was, it was deeply painful.

This great apostle who saw the resurrected Christ and was personally chosen for ministry by him, who performed mighty miracles in God's power, who established many churches, and who wrote much of the New Testament suffered more than we often call to mind. Paul was dearly loved by God, yet this friend of God suffered greatly.

Martyred Apostles

It's hard to read the Gospels without thinking about how amazing it must have been to be one of Jesus's twelve disciples. The opportunity to spend three years with the incarnate Son of God is hard for us to comprehend as those who have not seen him with our physical eyes or heard his voice with our physical ears. It's also incredible to think about the miraculous power that they were granted as apostles. Jesus gave them authority to "heal the sick, raise the dead, cleanse lepers, [and] cast out demons" (Matt. 10:8).

Yet most of these men, according to tradition, eventually died as martyrs. Of the remaining eleven after Judas's betrayal, ten were murdered for their faith in Christ, and one died in exile on Patmos (John). The one death that is recorded in Scripture is James's murder by Herod (see Acts 12:2). These men, dearly loved friends of God, suffered greatly.

As we behold the suffering of all these friends of God in Scripture, we understand why author Dan McCartney writes, "Rather than being a sign of *disfavor* with God, Job's suffering stood as a sign of God's *favor* and approval. . . . The fact of the matter is that in Scripture—most obviously in Job—it is often the person *favored* by God who suffers."[5] The term *favored* here does not mean that people who suffer more are God's "favorites" any more than those who suffer less in this life are his "favorites." God does not play favorites among his children in the sense of loving some more and others less. But he does display various manifestations of his grace, or favor, and that includes granting to some a deeper experience of suffering for the glory of God (see Phil. 1:29). And while it may certainly not feel like favor to us in this life, the vantage point from eternity will prove that this is so.

The Hebrews 11 Paradox

Hebrews 11 contains a jarring and—given the flow of the text—unexpected verse. In this famous chapter, we read about the marvelous acts of faith of various biblical figures throughout redemptive history, including Abel, Enoch, Noah, Abraham, Sarah, Jacob, Joseph, Moses, and more. In verses 33–35, we read that these men and women of faith

> conquered kingdoms, enforced justice, obtained promises, stopped the mouths of lions, quenched the power of fire, escaped the edge of the sword, were made strong out of weakness, became mighty in war, put foreign armies to flight. Women received back their dead by resurrection.

This sounds like something we can all get behind. Who wouldn't want a life of faith that conquers kingdoms, obtains promises, performs mighty deeds, and experiences the resurrection power of God to bring the dead back to life?

That's precisely why verse 35 is so disturbing. In the first half of the verse, we read, "Women received back their dead by resurrection." But then the chapter takes a very unexpected turn.

> Some were tortured, refusing to accept release, so that they might rise again to a better life. Others suffered mocking and flogging, and even chains and imprisonment. They were stoned, they were sawn in two, they were killed with the sword. They went about in skins of sheep and goats, destitute, afflicted, mistreated—of whom the world was not worthy—wandering about in deserts and mountains, and in dens and caves of the earth. (vv. 35–38)

It's stunning how quickly the script flips in verse 35. No new paragraph. Not even a transition word to signal that we're going from "good" to "bad." Just one continuous narrative of the people of God that moves from miraculous to macabre. Yet this passage is actually very good news for those experiencing comprehensive suffering.

Despite how we may feel, the truth is that we are not outside the circle of God's favor, care, and concern any more than the people described in Hebrews 11:35–38. Yes, from an earthly perspective, it may be that many of God's children are on the field trip while others are left in the classroom standing in the corner. But, just as we see in Hebrews 11, this does not mean that God plays favorites.

It can be easy to feel that way, but when we widen our perspective to others in Scripture and in history, we realize that God is not targeting us individually because of any cruelty or favoritism in him or because of any deficiency in us. He simply has different purposes for different people while showing perfect love toward every single son or daughter who belongs to him in Christ.

It's also true that sometimes we can't see and don't know the sufferings that people around us are facing. From the outside, it may look like they have "perfect" lives, and we may be tempted to envy them. Yet they, too, may be experiencing deep affliction that, for various reasons, they are not able to candidly share with others. Things are not always what they seem.

Some Were Delivered and Some Died

In Acts 12, we find the early church, led by the apostles, spreading the gospel of Jesus in obedience to his command.

> About that time Herod the king laid violent hands on some who belonged to the church. He killed James the brother of

John with the sword, and when he saw that it pleased the Jews, he proceeded to arrest Peter also. . . . And when he had seized him, he put him in prison, delivering him over to four squads of soldiers to guard him, intending after the Passover to bring him out to the people. So Peter was kept in prison, but earnest prayer for him was made to God by the church. (vv. 1–5)

The chapter goes on to tell that in the night, an angel of the Lord came to Peter in his cell, freed him, and led him out of the prison. Peter's response was, "Now I am sure that the Lord has sent his angel and rescued me from the hand of Herod and from all that the Jewish people were expecting" (v. 11). He then went to the house of Mary, where some of the Christians had gathered to pray. Understandably, when these believers saw Peter, they "were amazed" (v. 16).

This is an amazing story of divine intervention and deliverance. The church was praying for Peter, and God sent an angel to break him out of prison. Clearly, God's favor was upon Peter. But what we sometimes fail to notice in this passage is that another disciple of Jesus met with a very different providence. James was killed by Herod. Did the church pray that James would be miraculously delivered? We don't know. But here's the more important question: Did God love Peter more than he loved James? After all, both men, along with John, were in Jesus's "inner circle" of disciples, so it would seem that they were on equal footing before our Lord.

Because we're third-party observers of this story, it's easy for us to see that Peter's miraculous deliverance didn't mean that God loved Peter more and that James's murder didn't mean that God loved James less. They were both beloved apostles of God. Yet when it comes to our own lives, it's so much harder to interpret things with the same clarity. We see our own painful circumstances and others' amazing providences, and we wonder if God loves them more and us less. This story from Scripture helps us reorient our fearful and flawed conclusions.

And while it's true that in Acts 12, Peter received a miraculous delivery and James received a death sentence, Peter was later martyred as well. In the end, we can't say that James died but Peter was delivered. Because in the end, both men died, and both men, ultimately, were delivered.

The Secret Things Belong to God

So far, we've seen that when we look at God's friends in Scripture, our experience of comprehensive suffering falls right in line with many of their lives. While we may be the statistical outliers in our own churches and communities, we do belong to a larger, unseen group in which such suffering would be considered the norm rather than an anomaly (see 1 Peter 5:9). But at this point, it's natural to ask the following question: "*Why* does God ordain that some of his children will have relatively enjoyable, comfortable, and temporally blessed earthly lives, while others of his children will have relatively anguished, deprived, and tragic earthly lives?"

In the next chapter, we'll look at some passages in Scripture that give us a few possible answers to that question. But before we do, we must also acknowledge that we don't fully know exactly what God is doing or why. We can know some things, but we can't know all things. As Scripture says, "The secret things belong to the Lord our God, but the things that are revealed belong to us and to our children forever, that we may do all the words of this law" (Deut. 29:29). And God must have good reasons not to give us all the answers we want right now.

We don't like this as creatures—and it makes sense that we wouldn't. After all, we're made in the image of God. We naturally seek to understand the world around us. There's nothing wrong or sinful about wanting to understand what God's purposes are or to have our questions answered. It shows that we care about God and that we care about functioning properly in his world. The problem is that sometimes, we bump up against a boundary that shields us from the answers we want, from the secret things we want to be revealed. We reason that if God would just tell us the answer and explain why, we'd be able to endure our suffering so much better.

David Gibson observes,

> Part of being wise in this world is learning to accept that we have only very limited access to the big picture. . . . God is not being unkind to us by not sharing it; the point is that we are not built to understand the big picture, precisely because we live in time and God does not. If we could see the end from the beginning, and understand how a billion lives and a thousand generations and unspeakable sorrows and untold joys are all woven into a tapestry of perfect beauty, then we would be God.[6]

But even though God doesn't tell us all we want to know, he does tell us all we need to know. To be sure, in the context of comprehensive suffering, it can take a lot of time, tears, and trusted counselors to identify and cling to the revealed things that will enable us to keep walking with God in faith and obedience. Yet even in our weakness as we falter and struggle to cling to these truths, God is always clinging to us and upholding us with his strong hand.

You Follow Me

I've always been jostled by Jesus's response to Peter at the end of John's gospel. Jesus had just predicted that Peter would die a martyr's death, saying to him, "'Truly, truly, I say to you, when you were young, you used to dress yourself and walk wherever you wanted, but when you are old, you will stretch out your hands, and another will dress you and carry you where you do not want to go.' (This he said to show by what kind of death he was to glorify God)" (John 21:18–19).

Peter responds by asking Jesus what would happen to the apostle John: "Lord, what about this man?" (v. 21). Jesus answers, "If it is my will that he remain until I come, what is that to you? You follow me!" (v. 22). Jesus says the same to each one of us as we look at what's happening in our lives and compare it to others' lives. His response to Peter, and to us, is that it really shouldn't matter how God chooses to work in others' lives for his glory. No matter where the road he lays out for us may lead, the important thing is that we continue to follow him on it.

6

THE WAIT OF GLORY

I've always loved reading Christian biographies. The life stories of people who courageously lived for Christ, overcame formidable obstacles, and bore much fruit for the kingdom of God are inspiring. Some of us have dreamed of following in the footsteps of people like these, whether by becoming a missionary in a foreign land, starting a ministry to help a specific group of people, opening our homes to orphans and others in need, or any number of other ways that we might serve the church and the world.

But what happens when chronic suffering prevents us from fulfilling dreams like these? What happens when we desire to have a home open to others for hospitality, but we're living in someone else's house with no freedom to invite others over? What happens if our circumstances prevent us from leaving our current location and serving the Lord in another city, state, or country? What happens when the family we hoped to grow never materializes because we never got married, or because we live with chronic illness that doesn't allow us to have children? What happens when we long to minister to others but are rarely even able to make it to church?

It's easy to become disoriented in these circumstances. After all, the things that we desire are good things that would be honoring to God. Why, then, would he prevent us from doing the very things that his Word says are good or from fulfilling our desires to serve him with our lives? If we can't experience human flourishing in these ways, what motivation do we have to go on living when life just feels like a living death? And what's the point of enduring a greater degree of suffering in this life if everyone's slate just gets wiped clean in heaven and we all have the exact same experience in glory?

In this chapter, we'll explore how to navigate the reality of unfulfilled expectations, goals, and dreams in the face of chronic suffering. We'll examine why our seemingly small and pointless lives now matter so much in eternity, and we'll find reasons to endure and live each difficult day when so many of the best things in life are inaccessible to us.

Is God Wasting My Life?

A certain question inevitably crosses the mind of those living with chronic suffering. We're told that we should make the most of our lives and do all for the glory of God (see 1 Cor. 10:31). When faced with chronic suffering, we may be tempted to ask, "Is *God* wasting my life?"

In the Western world, we particularly esteem the value of production. What can we make? What can we do? What can we accomplish? This is all understandable, since part of being God's image bearers means that we desire to do valuable work, to subdue the earth, to make contributions, and to have our lives count for something beyond ourselves. But what has happened in our "hustle" culture, even in the church, is that we have begun to overestimate the value of production and underestimate the value of enduring in faith amid suffering.

I Just Want to Go Home

Given the fact that chronic suffering means we may not ever see our circumstances improved or restored this side of heaven, it's easy to see why it would be difficult for some of us to desire to remain on earth. Those of us facing chronic suffering typically have a greater longing to depart and be with the Lord, because the normal ties that bind people to earth may be absent from our lives or so painful to us that we see no reason to desire a long earthly life. Questions like these arise in our minds: Is it okay to just want to go and be with God instead? How do I view my life on earth? How can I endure when the suffering has impacted so many parts of what makes life really feel like *life* and my circumstances are unlikely to change?[1]

For those whose understandable desire to depart and be with the Lord (see Phil. 1:23) has morphed into contemplation of suicide, please do not wrestle alone with those thoughts. Reach out to trustworthy helpers—such as counselors, church leaders, family, and friends—who can navigate these deep waters with you.

What's the Point?

It's also natural to ask, "What's the point of my suffering?" After all, we can endure difficult things much better if we understand the purpose of the suffering and the beneficial outcome. A woman in labor may experience great pain during her delivery, but she endures because she knows the purpose of the pain: It will result in the blessing of a child. But compare the pain of a woman in labor to that of someone who lives with chronic pain, and the storyline is much different. The pregnant woman's pain is temporary and will culminate in the immediate blessing for which she longs (the exception being women who birth stillborn babies, or babies with severe medical complications, or babies who die in infancy—this is its own form of suffering). But people with chronic pain face ongoing physical affliction every day with no end in sight, and there's no certain earthly blessing born from it.

All those who endure some form of chronic suffering must rely on a hope of blessing and a hope of relief that is longer-range than immediate temporal joys. But do the pain, suffering, and loss make a difference at the end of the day? If all believers are going to end up in glory in the new heavens and new earth, is there any value or purpose in the greater degree of suffering that some experience? According to Scripture, the answer is yes. It really does matter. Let's see how the Bible speaks to our questions as we wonder whether God is wasting our lives, as we desire to go and be with him, and as we ask if there's any point to our chronic suffering.

Temporal Affliction Prepares Future Glory

Hope can hurt, and so we can be tempted to kill it. When we try to keep going amid chronic suffering, praying and hoping that God will bring temporal relief and restoration, we can become disillusioned, discouraged, depressed, or despairing when nothing changes. And the truth is, our hopes for earthly improvements aren't promised and may never materialize. If that's the case, how can we endure our earthly lives when relief and restoration are guaranteed only at our death? If this world is just treading water until we go to be with the Lord, and if this world really doesn't matter for the next world, then what would motivate us to keep going with any sense of purpose or hope?

In doctrinally sound churches, we typically receive solid biblical teaching on the connection between this world and the next when it comes to sin and judgment. Those who do not trust in Christ will be judged for their sins and condemned to hell. Those who do trust in Christ will enter the glories of heaven through his merits, as well as receive gracious rewards for their acts of love toward God and others on this earth. Yet when it comes to suffering, we sometimes separate this world and the next. Or, if we do acknowledge a connection between the two, it's in a more general sense that lumps all believers together. That is, we tend to think that since we all suffer on some level, we'll all attain the same weight of glory.

But this isn't the case. Scripture connects suffering in this world to our experience of the next world. It connects our present life with our future life. Why? Because the bad now will actually make the good better. To say it another way, this world and the next are not hermetically sealed off from each other. What happens *now* has implications for what will be *then*. That's why we can endure this life: Because it's preparing future glory.

In other words, heaven isn't a cosmic do-over that wipes everyone's earthly slate clean and gives us all the exact same experiences, rewards, opportunities, and responsibilities in the new heavens and new earth. If that were the case, it would be very hard to be motivated to persevere in a life filled with chronic suffering. But, as theologian R.C. Sproul understood, "right now counts forever."[2] Everything that happens today has eternal significance. Let's see how Scripture testifies that our temporal affliction now is preparing us for future glory then.

Second Corinthians 4:16–17 says,

> So we do not lose heart. Though our outer self is wasting away, our inner self is being renewed day by day. For this light momentary affliction *is preparing for us* an eternal weight of glory beyond all comparison.

Note the wording here. Paul is not simply saying that this light momentary affliction will eventually *turn into* glory. Glory doesn't come after affliction in the way that there might be a happy ending to a hard story. The truth is much grander: The affliction we experience now in this life actually *produces* the particular weight of glory that we will receive in the new heavens and new earth.

The Greek word translated into English as "preparing" in 2 Corinthians 4:17, sometimes translated as "producing," means "to cause a state or condition" or to "bring about."[3] In other words, there is an indelible link between suffering now and glory then. This world will influence that world. The temporal will echo into and shape the eternal. This means that every second of our suffering matters. Every tear shed, every groan uttered, every act of worship rendered, every grief endured, is preparing future glory for us, as well as preparing us for that future glory. This is good news for weary sufferers who wonder why endurance is worth it.

Jesus acknowledged this connection during his earthly ministry. He says to the Twelve in Matthew 19:28–30,

> Truly, I say to you, in the new world, when the Son of Man will sit on his glorious throne, you who have followed me will also sit on twelve thrones, judging the twelve tribes of Israel. And everyone who has left houses or brothers or sisters or father or mother or children or lands, for my name's sake, will receive a hundredfold and will inherit eternal life. But many who are first will be last, and the last first.

While we don't know exactly what this will look like, there is a kingdom principle at play here in which those who suffered more and had less in this life will be bestowed with greater glory in the next life.

In Matthew 20, Jesus tells his disciples for a third time that he will be turned in to the religious authorities, condemned to death, and handed over to the gentiles to be crucified. Then the mother of James and John asks Jesus to bestow glory on her sons: "Say that these two sons of mine are to sit, one at your right hand and one at your left, in your kingdom" (v. 21). Notice that Jesus doesn't respond with a yes or a no. Rather, he responds by reiterating this kingdom principle that connects suffering and glory: "You do not know what you are asking. Are you able to drink the cup that I am to drink?" (v. 22). Here, Jesus notes a connection. There is no shortcut to glory. Great glory comes only as a result of great suffering. You can't have one without the other.

Therefore, we need to reclaim an expanded view of eternal rewards that doesn't limit the reward recipients to type A, go-getter Christians with well-known ministries and platforms. These bear a legitimate type of fruit for the kingdom and will be rewarded. But fruit also falls into another category: the fruit of character. This is displayed in the tenacious faith, courage, humility, and perseverance that it takes to live a hidden life, confined or alone with no ability to serve the Lord in the ways that one longs to. This fruit is dazzling in glory.

Additionally, we read in 1 Peter 4:13, "But rejoice insofar as you share Christ's sufferings, that you may also rejoice and be glad when his glory is revealed." Here we see a link not only between suffering and glory but between suffering, glory, and joy. The more one shares in Christ's suffering on this earth, the greater one's capacity for joy on the day that his glory is revealed. More weeping in this life will actually produce more rejoicing in the next. David Gibson notes the following regarding the link between life now and life then:

> The times of my life are not the only times there are. There is a time to be born and a time to die, and there is a time for judgment. One of the ways we learn to live by preparing to die is by realizing that death means judgment and that this is a good thing. It gives my present actions meaning and weight, and it gives my experienced losses and injustices a voice in God's presence. What is past may be past, but what is past is not forgotten to God, and because he is in charge and lives forever, one day all will be well. Every single thing that happens will have its day in court.[4]

The Weight of Glory

There is a connection between suffering in this world and glory. This motivates us in chronic suffering, even when there's no hope that circumstances will change in this life. But what exactly is meant by the term *glory*? We know that glory is a good thing, and we probably have an impression of what we think it means. But what does the Bible mean when it talks about glory?

The Hebrew word for "glory," *kabod*, usually refers to weightiness or substance. There is a gravitas, a significance, a resplendence, to glory. We might even say that the Bible is a chronicle of the glory story: It reveals to us the character and acts of the brilliantly shining, incomparably weighty and significant God. And while there is a glory that rightly belongs to God alone, Scripture is clear that there is also a type of glory that he gifts to his people. As Jesus suffered before entering glory, walking through Gethsemane and experiencing death at Golgotha, we, too, will experience suffering on our way to glory. The apostle Paul teaches this when he says, "And if [we are] children [of God], then heirs—heirs of God and fellow heirs with Christ, provided we suffer with him in order that we may also be glorified with him" (Rom. 8:17).

While we don't know exactly what this glory will look like, we can say that greater suffering in this life will produce greater glory in the next and that such glory will be wonderful beyond our comprehension. Matthew Henry notes, "Jesus Christ will appear again in glory, and, when he does so, the saints will appear with him, and their graces will appear illustrious; and the more they have been tried the more bright they will then appear. The trial will soon be over, but the glory, honour, and praise will last to eternity. This should reconcile you to your present afflictions: *they work for you a far more exceeding and eternal weight of glory.*"[5] We see how this principle is true even now on a human level. It is often those who have suffered the most who speak with the depth, wisdom, and weight that suffering can produce.

Not only can the suffering we experience in this life influence the glory we will experience in the next life; our suffering can also bring glory to God and to others. Paul says to the Ephesian church, "I ask you not to lose heart over what I am suffering for you, which is your glory" (Eph. 3:13). While the nature of the glory Paul refers to in this passage isn't clear, the fact remains that in God's providence, the suffering that Paul experienced produced glory for the Ephesian believers. While it may be easy for us to believe that our suffering couldn't possibly contribute to others' glory—especially if our suffering causes us to be physically or relationally isolated from other people, or both—the truth is that we have no idea how God might be using our lives to glorify himself and to produce glory in others.

The Story Sufferers Tell

There is good news for chronic sufferers. Our affliction now really does matter, because enduring by faith will produce greater glory for us in eternity. God is not wasting our lives; rather, he's allowing us to invest more deeply in the life we'll one day have forever. This gives us a reason to keep living today even if our circumstances never get better, because what we do now really does matter for our future. There is a point to our pain, and one day we'll see how God uses all the bad to produce a good that otherwise wouldn't have been. But there's one more aspect of chronic suffering that deserves our attention, especially in a world that's focused on achievement, success, and external manifestations of value. Let's look now at the story that only sufferers can tell.

The Old Testament prophet Habakkuk faced deeply difficult circumstances. His book is unique in that it doesn't record any of his addresses to the people of Israel. Instead, "the book is rather a record of the prophet's own struggles with questions of faith."[6] Appalled by the corruption of Judah in his day, Habakkuk was troubled by God's seeming reluctance to step in and act. But the Lord's answer only produced more confusion, disorientation, and distress for Habakkuk when God revealed that he was going to use the wicked Chaldeans to judge Judah. The Lord responded to Habakkuk's dismay by telling him that the righteous would live by faith as they trusted that God is a righteous judge who will ultimately destroy the proud and redeem those who wait for him (see Hab. 2:2–4).

The book closes with famous lines from the prophet:

Though the fig tree should not blossom,
    nor fruit be on the vines,
the produce of the olive fail
    and the fields yield no food,
the flock be cut off from the fold
    and there be no herd in the stalls,
yet I will rejoice in the Lord;
    I will take joy in the God of my salvation.
God, the Lord, is my strength;
    he makes my feet like the deer's;
    he makes me tread on my high places. (3:17–19)

Because his words are so poetic, we can fail to see how dire the circumstances he portrays really are. He's talking about a lack of flourishing and the presence of affliction, hunger, and poverty. To be able to rejoice in the Lord in those circumstances is impossible without supernatural empowerment. Something special is happening here.

In other words, this is the story that only sufferers can tell: God is worthy of our devotion and praise even if our lives are bad and our circumstances are horrible. In that way, those who endure chronic suffering can glorify God in a unique way. Joni Eareckson Tada, who has spent most of her life as a quadriplegic, says this:

> [God's] melody—His incomparable, heavenly, impossibly beautiful music—somehow comes into its own when it emanates from a broken, battered, but fully yielded human vessel.
>
> It's music that can only come from particular instruments, broken in particular ways, and yielded with particular humility. I also believe it brings God glory in a way that is completely unique on earth or in the heavens. And that's a thought that keeps me going, too.
>
> Music played in the dark may have more spiritual power than music performed in the safe and pleasing light of a daylight concert or a well-lighted concert hall.[7]

A Hidden Life

Sometimes, if suffering isn't visible to many people, or if suffering results in relatively few relationships or social interactions, it can be easy to think that walking by faith and living in obedience to the Lord don't matter as much. After all, we're used to hearing stories about how God can use our suffering to bring unbelievers to faith in Christ. But what if you're alone in your suffering? Is there any point to your suffering if you're living a hidden life?

In Luke 8:17, Jesus says, "For nothing is hidden that will not be made manifest, nor is anything secret that will not be known and come to light." When we think of hidden things being exposed, we usually think of the secret sins people hide that God will one day expose to the light. And this is true. But the converse is true as well: The ordinary, faithful, day-to-day actions of hidden, suffering believers will one day be exposed to the light at the judgment seat of Christ; the hidden prayers and tears, the tiny but monumental acts of faith when life is crushing, the songs sung to the Lord in the dark in the middle of the night, will be acknowledged by him. The book of Ecclesiastes concurs, concluding the Preacher's words in this way:

> The end of the matter; all has been heard. Fear God and keep his commandments, for this is the whole duty of man. For God will bring every deed into judgment, with every secret thing, whether good or evil. (12:13–14)

But there's even more. Not only will what is hidden now be revealed one day, but your suffering has an audience in the here and now, even if you're in a room completely alone. How can this be? Earlier, we noted how the temporal and eternal are not separate from each other. The temporal has implications for and flows into the future. In a similar way, the natural world that we can see with our eyes here on earth is not separate from the invisible spiritual realm of God, the angels, the saints in heaven, Satan, and the demons.

This truth is especially precious for those whose comprehensive and chronic suffering involves isolation. Does your faithfulness matter as much when other people aren't there to witness it and have their faith strengthened (for believers) or be drawn to Christ (for unbelievers)? Tada provides helpful insight on this point: "Here on earth, we're being observed by both the sons and daughters of God. . . . And beyond these earthly eyes, there are other eyes in the spirit realm—both angelic and demonic—who observe and take note whether or not we trust our God in the crucible of trials and affliction."[8]

The apostle Paul acknowledges this intersection of the natural and spiritual worlds when he says to Timothy, "In the presence of God and of Christ Jesus and of the elect angels I charge you to keep these rules without prejudging, doing nothing from partiality" (1 Tim. 5:21). There's a sense in which our lives are 24-7 "reality shows" in the spiritual realms, as both the angels of God and the demons of hell witness our everyday trials and everyday choices.

The film *A Hidden Life* presents the story of Franz Jägerstätter, an Austrian farmer who refused to swear an oath of allegiance to Hitler and fight for the German army in World War II.[9] Pressured by his neighbors (including the church and its leaders), imprisoned, and brought to trial, he kept refusing to sign the oath and was executed by the Nazis in 1943. In the film, a judge wonders why Jägerstätter remains so steadfast to his convictions given the dire consequences for not signing the oath. He indicates that there is no point in Jägerstätter's holding fast to his beliefs. After all, what he was doing wouldn't change the war's outcome, and his sacrifice wouldn't produce any fruit or change in the world. The judge said that no one would even know about Jägerstätter.

But as we've seen, nothing is really hidden. Therefore, our life matters, our faith matters, and our obedience matters more than we know. And because all these things are true, we can endure as God, who sees us, sustains us in faith day by day.

A Light and Momentary Long Time

When we read books or hear sermons about the sufferings of this life, the emphasis is sometimes placed on the fact that these sufferings are brief when compared to eternity. That's true. We saw in 2 Corinthians 4:17 that such afflictions are described as "light" and "momentary" in comparison to eternity. First Peter 1:6 says that these troubles last "for a little while." It can be helpful to reorient our thinking to these truths. Remembering that the endurance we must display in this life is only a dot on the line of eternity can provide hope and encouragement.

At the same time, this truth might cause us to wonder: Are we just supposed to keep a stiff upper lip and tell ourselves and others that our heavy and long affliction doesn't matter? That it's not really that heavy or that long? Tada provides this insight: "What does God think about four decades of paralysis? I got my answer not long ago when I read Joshua 24:7, where the Lord recounts for His children all the trials they endured after they left Egypt. He tenderly reminds them, 'Then you lived in the desert *for a long time.*'"[10] In our efforts to stand by the biblical truth that when compared with eternity, our suffering is light and momentary, let's not forget an equally precious biblical truth. God does not minimize the weight and length of our affliction. There's a sense in which our momentary suffering lasts for a long time—both to us and to the One who loves us.

Part 3

Living with Suffering

7

WEEPING IN HURT

Years ago, I participated in a fitness class where the instructor had us balance on one foot. Most of us could do this, though some were wobbling and shaking more than others. Then she told us to close our eyes while balancing on one foot. As it turns out, it's exponentially more difficult to try to balance on one foot when you can't see. There's something about being in the dark that makes even simple tasks much harder. And in this scenario, we weren't even trying to walk or move around. On one foot in the dark, that would have been nearly impossible.

The same is true in comprehensive and chronic suffering. We can often feel as though we're in the dark, and if we want to keep moving forward, we're going to need two vital "legs" for our journey: lamenting and rejoicing. Both are necessary if we want to keep our balance and continue our journey heavenward. Scripture does not portray a godly life as rejoicing to the exclusion of lamenting, nor as lamenting to the exclusion of rejoicing. Rather, both can be evidence of godly wisdom, and both are seen in the perfect earthly life of wisdom personified: our Lord Jesus Christ.

Lamenting and rejoicing are requisite components of faithful Christian living in a fallen world as we not only live our own lives but also experience the joys and sorrows of those around us in the body of Christ. Because we are spiritual brothers and sisters, our joys and sorrows should be greater than the sum total of our own personal experience. In a sense, we should experience a thousand joys and a thousand sorrows as we are united to one another through our union with Christ.

Lamenting and rejoicing. Weeping and laughing. Grieving and celebrating. This is the biblical pattern, and however paradoxical it may seem, this is God's path for us as we follow him, lamenting and rejoicing as we limp heavenward by his grace.

Why Should We Lament?

Lament may be an unfamiliar practice for many Christians. This is especially the case in the West, where expressions of grief are sometimes swept under the rug or plastered over with superficial biblical platitudes. But because we live in a fallen world, something has gone awry if we view rejoicing in the face of suffering, loss, and death as the only appropriate expression of faith.

Living by faith includes lament. Why? Because we believe that God's original intent for creation was a world filled with wholeness, peace, and flourishing, often referred to in the Bible by the Hebrew word *shalom*. But sin and its consequences have wreaked havoc on our world—fracturing wholeness, disrupting peace, and thwarting flourishing. In Christ, that shalom has begun to be restored, yet we live in the "already / not yet," waiting for the Lord to return and to fully and finally restore the cosmos. Because our faith is rooted in this framework of creation, fall, redemption, and consummation, we lament the ways in which sin has distorted God's world and brought great suffering upon the earth.

Yet we also have true hope as believers. While worldly hope is simply wishing for a positive future outcome but not knowing whether it will occur, Christian hope is rooted in the truthfulness of God as expressed in his Word. As a result, we can be confident that everything he has promised will surely come to pass.

Because of these realities, Christians alone have a true and lasting hope in the face of affliction and loss, but we should also be the ones who see and feel the profound horrors of a broken world the most deeply, resulting in faith-filled lament to the Lord.

What Is Lament?

Author Mark Vroegop defines lament as "a prayer in pain that leads to trust. Throughout the Scriptures, lament gives voice to the strong emotions that believers feel because of suffering. It wrestles with the struggles that surface."[1] When suffering and loss are more than just a season, lament will be (and should be) ongoing. In this way, lament helps us maintain spiritual and emotional health by preventing a dangerous buildup of thoughts and emotions in our hearts. Biblical lament creates a conduit through which we can channel these things into the very presence of God.

It is instructive to note that approximately one-third of the book of Psalms comprises psalms of lament. Clearly, God desires for his people to bring their heartache, their tears, their confusion, their weariness, and their questions to him, for in Scripture he provides us with the very blueprint for such laments. Zack Eswine writes, "What God created and purposed was legitimate and original good. To lose this good is pain. There are things worth crying about. . . . Speaking what troubles us needn't indicate our immaturity. Sometimes only the mature have the capacity to resist denial or pretense and to admit things as they truly are."[2] Godly lament is a sign of wisdom and spiritual maturity. Further, Kelly Kapic notes the potential spiritual danger of life without lament: "If we do not restore space for lament in our individual and corporate church life, our suffering will drive us not only away from others but away from God himself."[3]

How might we learn to lament our comprehensive and chronic suffering to the Lord? What examples in Scripture can we look to as guides? Though many resources on lament point us (understandably) to the Psalms, in this chapter we will use the book of Job as our primary guide for lamenting deep and ongoing losses, with the Psalms as a secondary reference. Job's laments give divinely inspired voice to some of the darkest human experiences possible. As such, our deepest agonies can find expression as we share in Job's words. Though we may feel utterly alone in our comprehensive and chronic suffering, we find in Job a companion who understands the complexities of both our external circumstances and our internal anguish.

Dignity and Dehumanization

Comprehensive and chronic suffering can strip us of dignity in many ways—not in the sense that we lose our dignity as God's image bearers but in the sense that our *experience* of living as image bearers with dignity has changed. The opposite of dignity—of being free to function fully as an image bearer of God—is dehumanization. As the word implies, dehumanized people feel as though they have become something less than human. Dehumanization is deeply disorienting and disturbing, and it can be hard to put the experience into words. The book of Job helps us in this regard. In chapters 29–30, Job chronicles his radical transition from dignity to dehumanization by comparing his life before and after his suffering began.

Before his plunge into suffering and loss, Job experienced God's presence, blessing, and friendship (see 29:1–5). Despite his riches, his relationship with God was his greatest treasure. He was blessed with a spouse and many children (see v. 5). He was a financially prosperous man (see v. 6) who received honor and respect from others and acted as a leader in the community (see vv. 7–10, 21–25). In those golden days, Job served the weak from his position of strength (see vv. 11–17).

But in chapter 30, his suffering reverses all the blessings described in chapter 29. Rather than experiencing God's presence, blessing, and friendship, Job now experiences terror (see 30:15) and affliction (see v. 16), saying that he had been cast into the mire by God (see v. 19). Instead of enjoying the friendship of God, Job now perceives God as an enemy who is against him (see vv. 20–22). Instead of being surrounded by family and friends, Job is now alone (see v. 29). His prosperity has dried up and vanished (see v. 15). Instead of occupying a place of honor within the community, Job is now dishonored and disrespected by his community (see vv. 1, 9–10). And rather than serving the weak from his position of strength, Job descends into weakness, now living as one who needs help from others rather than as one who can help others (see v. 28).

Most people who experience comprehensive and chronic suffering can relate to at least one of these losses, and probably many more. What was once a precious, safe, and secure relationship with the Lord can turn into a terrifying perception of God as a hostile enemy rather than a loving friend.

Maybe the social connections and relationships that once enriched your life have vanished, leaving you isolated. Or the ability to work and earn income has become difficult or impossible, leaving you laden with financial stress and simply trying to survive. Perhaps the opportunities you once had to use your gifts and talents in your career, church, and community have been taken away, and you feel like you can no longer do meaningful work as an image bearer. And perhaps worst of all, maybe you can no longer serve the weak as one who is strong. Instead, you've learned the terror of being the needy and weak one, dependent on the attention and ability of the strong for your very survival. Experiencing just one of these losses can be devastating; experiencing them all can lead to a dark desolation of the soul.

In the sections that follow, we will explore various facets of Job's dehumanization in his comprehensive and chronic suffering. After each section, a sample prayer of lament is provided to show how you might lament various losses and griefs before the Lord. The laments can be repeated as written, or they can serve as jumping-off points to write or speak personalized laments that best fit your particular circumstances. Because developing a deeper trust in the Lord in dark circumstances is a process, you probably won't suddenly be filled with unshakable faith after repeating a few sentences. Accordingly, each lament ends with a petition that God would increase our faith and help us to believe that what he says is true.

Sometimes it can be helpful to read and repeat a lament that is already written, especially if you feel overwhelmed by your emotions in the moment and need something to ground you. You are also free to voice extemporaneous laments to the Lord, lifting your voice and heart and grief to him. And sometimes, you may not even be able to recite a pre-written lament or adequately convey yourself to the Lord with your own words. Sometimes you may need to simply weep before him with groans, trusting that the Holy Spirit will translate your Godward groans into petitions as he groans on your behalf (see Rom. 8:26–27).

Isolated and Invisible

One of the most prominent ways we can experience dehumanization is by becoming seemingly invisible to others, unseen and unheard. It's as though we simply don't exist anymore. Job experienced this in both his relationships with others and his relationship with God. Job says that God has "made desolate all [his] company" (Job 16:7). The psalmists pick up this theme of isolation and invisibility in deep affliction, saying that no one is there to help them (see Ps. 22:11), that they are forgotten like those who are dead (see 31:12), that no one notices them or cares for them (see 142:4), and that they are shunned by their companions (see 88:8, 18).

It's bad enough to be unseen and unheard by others, but it's excruciating to feel as though we are unseen and unheard by God himself. Job experienced this too. He says that God has hidden his face from him (see Job 13:24). He calls to God for help, but there is no response (see 19:7). The psalmists also echo this perception of being unseen and unheard by God. They say that God is standing far away from them and hiding himself in times of trouble (see Ps. 10:1). They feel forgotten by God and have no sense of his presence (see 13:1–2). They feel forsaken and say that God is not answering their prayers (see 22:1–2). They say that God is hiding his face from them and forgetting their affliction (see 44:24) and that he has cast their souls away (see 88:14).

O Lord, I'm so profoundly and painfully lonely. I feel invisible to you and to the world. Over time, it seems that my friends have forgotten me in my affliction. Everyone rushes about, busy with their own lives, families, careers, and pursuits. I am alone on so many birthdays, holidays, and days in between. Few care for me or my welfare, call to check on me, or invite me to fellowship. When I go out, I often feel alone, even in a crowd, because so few people know or understand the realities of my suffering. Sometimes it feels as though I've already died and been forgotten. No one notices me, no one is a refuge for me, and no one cares for my soul. This covers me with shame and drowns me in fear.

I feel invisible even to you, O Lord. I call out to you, but my prayers go unanswered. It's like you've hidden your face from me. When I need you the most, it feels like you're standing far away or have forgotten me and my affliction. O Lord, it fills me with grief and terror to feel so isolated from and invisible to you.

Remind me that you are with me and that I am never ultimately alone, even if all others forsake me and I don't sense your presence with me. Remind me that even though I feel isolated and invisible, your Word promises that I'm not—that because of Jesus, you will never forsake me and your Holy Spirit indwells me. Strengthen me to walk by faith and help me remember that just because I can't see or feel the sun on a cloudy day doesn't mean that the sun's not there. Lord, please part the clouds in my soul and preserve my soul as I trust in you, be it ever so weakly. Keep me in your strong hand until the glorious day comes when I am never isolated or invisible again. Amen.

Tightly Trapped

Being or feeling tightly trapped is another way that we can experience dehumanization in comprehensive and chronic suffering. Job experienced this when the hedge of protection that God had previously placed around him to shield him from harm (see 1:10) became a hedge that trapped him inside a horrible nightmare, in a tightly confined space from which there was no escape. What was once a fence protecting his life, property, and well-being became an impenetrable concrete wall that cut off anything good from entering his life.

Job says that he is hedged in by God (Job 3:23) and feels targeted, even hunted, by him (see 10:16). He feels as though he is in prison (see 12:14). God has walled up his way, and there is no hope of escape (see 19:8). The psalmists also speak of God's putting them in a deep, dark pit (see Ps. 88:6) and shutting them in so that there is no escape (see v. 8).

O Lord, it feels like I'm suffocating, trapped in a tiny box that I can't escape. I feel like I'm living in a hallway filled with locked doors, unable to open one and enjoy a better life. It seems that no matter how hard I try, you keep me trapped while others move freely, able to live and serve in the ways they desire. I grow so weary of the failed attempts to better my circumstances that sometimes I just want to give up.

It feels like you've walled up my way and shut me into a deep pit that I can't climb out of. My life keeps shrinking and getting smaller and smaller as time goes by, and the dreams I once had die a little more each day.

O Lord, remind me that your ways with your people are often mysterious. Encourage me in the truth of your Word. You do not waste the lives of your people, but you have purpose in all things, even when the pain feels pointless. Help me faithfully walk the hard path you have laid out for me, tight and constricted as it might be, and fill me with hope that this tight path will lead to a broad place of glory and delight. There, I will roam freely in the new heavens and new earth, filled with endless opportunities to fully live for your glory without suffering and sin. Amen.

Harassed and Helpless

A sense of terror and helplessness often arises when comprehensive and chronic suffering consumes what we hold dear and we are defenseless to stop it or change it. Job feels as though God himself is the one harassing and terrorizing him. Because of this, Job is miserable and longs for death (see Job 3:20–21). He dreads God's power and sovereignty (see 23:13–17) and finds him terrifying (see 6:4). Job even asks God to kill him because he knows that he is too weak and helpless to keep going—he doesn't have the resources to endure (see

vv. 8–13). His life is like a slave's, filled with months of emptiness and nights of misery (see 7:1–3); his nights are plagued with terrifying nightmares (see v. 14). He says that God won't even give him a chance to swallow his spit before striking him again with affliction (see v. 19). Job begs God to withdraw his hand from him (see 13:21) and asks why God has hidden his face from him and counted him as his enemy (see v. 24).

Job describes this sense of God's harassment in violent and graphic language.

> I was at ease, and he broke me apart;
>> he seized me by the neck and dashed me to pieces;
> he set me up as his target;
>> his archers surround me.
> He slashes open my kidneys and does not spare;
>> he pours out my gall on the ground.
> He breaks me with breach upon breach;
>> he runs upon me like a warrior. (Job 16:12–14)

The author of Psalm 88 speaks similarly, saying that God has put him in a deep, dark pit (see v. 6). He is terrified, helpless, and destroyed by God's assaults, which surround him like a flood and back him into a corner (see vv. 15–17). Psalm 142 perhaps best describes the experience of harassment and helplessness by simply saying that there's no safe place to go—"No refuge remains to me"—and that there's no one to help the helpless—"Look to the right and see: there is none who takes notice of me; . . . no one cares for my soul" (v. 4).

> O Lord, I feel terrified and helpless. I am weak and tiny, and the world is filled with many evils and dangers. So many bad

things have happened to me that I'm always waiting for the next wave of calamity to knock me down. It's all so difficult and miserable that sometimes I long for death. I know that you are sovereign, but sometimes that makes me afraid of you. Why have you ordained so many awful things to befall me?

I feel too weak and helpless to keep going, and I'm afraid of what the future holds. Perhaps I could endure these terrors if I had help and support from other people, but I don't. I'm afraid that no one will be there in my time of need. And I don't feel help or support from you, Lord.

Please grant me comfort rather than terror in your sovereignty. Remind me that Satan, my enemy, is the one who harasses me and has ill intent toward me. Your Word says that you are a loving Father to your children. Teach me to find comfort in your ways as I look to your Word for the truth about your heart toward your children, even when you ordain affliction for them. Strengthen me in the truth that even if I am helpless on a human level and have no one to come to my aid, your plans for me cannot be thwarted, and even all the bad things will lead to my ultimate and eternal joy in you. Please comfort me as I look forward to the day when there will be no more tears, fears, or terrors anymore. Amen.

Midlife Meltdown

If comprehensive and chronic suffering hits you in midlife, it can be a shock to the system. At what should be the high point of your life—when you think you can grow and succeed and accomplish the most—you are struck down in your prime and perhaps even lose everything you have been building. Especially in the context of chronic illness, it may feel like you are trapped in the life of someone far older. While, in normal circumstances, life gradually slows down and is taken away from us the older we get, midlife desolation takes us by complete surprise as it strikes us down in the middle of our days. Job knew what this was like.

He sees his life passing him by:

> My days are swifter than a runner;
>   they flee away; they see no good.
> They go by like skiffs of reed,
>   like an eagle swooping on the prey. (Job 9:25–26)

Instead of the strength of middle age, Job is shriveled up like an old man (see 16:8). It's as though his life is over, but his physical body hasn't yet gotten the memo. Thus, he hangs suspended like a ghost in the land of the living, forced to exist in a kind of living death. He says, "My spirit is broken; my days are extinct; the graveyard is ready for me" (17:1) and "My days are past; my plans are broken off, the desires of my heart" (v. 11).

It feels like his life has ended. He has no hope of a future in his earthly life. Christopher Ash writes, "If he tries to look forward, all he can see is a blank wall of hopelessness as his affections and longings are turned back upon themselves in despair. . . . The prime of Job's life is passing him by with no achievements, no delight, no relationships, no hope. Another birthday, another year of misery gone."[4] The psalmists echo these sentiments, describing their lives as spent with sorrow and their years with sighing (see Ps. 31:10). They are the living dead (see 88:4–5); their lives have been cut off right in the middle (see 102:23–24).

While some experience a midlife meltdown like Job, others experience profound suffering that began at a young age, perhaps even from birth. Scripture speaks to these circumstances as well. For example, the writer of Psalm 88 notes, "Afflicted and close to death from my youth up, I suffer your terrors; I am helpless" (v. 15). And Psalm 129 opens with the words, "Greatly have they afflicted me from my youth" (v. 1). When we experience comprehensive and chronic suffering that begins at a young age, our laments are less about the loss of things in midlife and more about the pain of things that never were.

O Lord, my heart is downcast as I remember what my life used to be and what it has now become. I used to feel the light of your countenance on me. Life wasn't perfect, but it felt like there was a balance between blessings and trials, between joys and sorrows. And then, all the good seemed to be snatched away from me overnight. Everything seemed to fall apart right in the middle of the story, and I don't understand why.

I thought that things would get better, but they haven't. It feels like I spend my life surviving rather than thriving. You seem far away, and I have no sense of your presence. Deep down, I wonder if you hate me or if I don't belong to you. I feel like a ghost in the land of the living, desperately wanting to live for you and serve in the ways my heart desires. But instead, I'm like a half-human, struggling to get through another day. My hopes and plans have perished. Life has become a labored sigh, and my dreams have died.

Lord, have mercy on me. Strengthen me according to your Word. Free me with your truth. Empower me through your Spirit. Guard me from the Evil One. Give me sustaining grace and comfort me in my affliction, that I may courageously live for you even in deep and dark places. Amen.

Bad News Before Good News

Oftentimes, when pastors teach us about sharing the gospel, they say that we must share the bad news of sin before the good news of salvation. By this, they mean that we can't ignore that the bad exists, for the good makes sense only when we understand the bad. Yet while many Christians understand this principle in the context of human sin, we often fail to apply it in the context of human suffering. One might wonder why we've spent so much time focusing on the story of Job, such deep desolation of soul, and the importance of lament. There are two reasons.

First, God does still call some people, even on this side of the cross, to experience severe affliction, and if we want to endure, we must find a way forward through the pages of Scripture. If our lived experience can't be connected to God's Word, then we won't see how our stories fit into God's story, and we can find no place for ourselves in God's Word or God's world. What we need most amid such suffering is the assurance that our experience doesn't mean that we don't belong to God or that we have been abandoned by him, even though it may feel as though we are.

That's why God's Word must lay down the footprints that we seek to follow and serve as the grid through which we understand our experiences. Therefore, these dark words are actually a precious gift to sufferers, telling us that other believers have felt and experienced what we have. Our experience—no matter how extreme—still fits into God's story. And though our *perception* of God's abandonment or hostility is real—just as it was to Job and the psalmists—the *reality* is that we are still in God's hand and belong to him just as much as these other believers in Scripture did, even if it doesn't feel true at times.

Another reason why we must be honest about the bad news of our suffering is that our suffering is real and true. We would be denying reality to speak and act otherwise. Say, for example, that a person discovers black mold in their home. One approach to the situation would be to paint or wallpaper over it, trying to create the illusion that everything is fine because it looks good on the surface. The other approach is to acknowledge that something bad is happening and to seek to understand the full extent of how deep and far the damage runs. That way, after soberly assessing how bad things are, the person can seek to remediate the damage and bring a truer and deeper restoration to the home.

Weep with Those Who Weep

Not only must we lament our own losses and pain as we journey through life, but we are to lament with others as well. Romans 12:15 tells us to "weep with those who weep." Many who encounter comprehensive and chronic suffering find that they become much more compassionate toward others than they were before they personally experienced deep affliction. Though we might wish that God had taught us this lesson in a less painful way, the fact remains that it is a good thing when we grow in compassion.

People living with comprehensive and chronic suffering often feel as though they can't minister to others in the ways they used to because of their limitations. This may be true. But as the Lord gives us opportunity and ability, we can be a listening ear and a comforting presence as we sit together with others on the ash heap of life and mourn with them the things that should be that are not and the things that are that should not be. In so doing, we participate in the ministry of the body of Christ and serve our Lord himself. And as we more deeply understand and embrace the truths we've covered in chapters 2–6, we might even find ourselves in a position to comfort others as we have been comforted (see 2 Cor. 1:4).

8

REJOICING IN HOPE

For as long as I can remember, a painting hung on the wall at the halfway point of the stairs in my grandparents' house. For years, every time I walked up or down the stairs, I was confronted with what I thought was a horribly ugly piece of art. Inside a thick, dark brown frame, a scene of survival and despair was depicted. The painting shows four men in a small boat about the size of a canoe facing a fierce storm on the ocean. The waters are dark and menacing. The boat and the men inside of it are in the center of the canvas, and our eyes are immediately drawn to their struggle. Three men look toward us, their faces visibly exhausted from rowing through the dangerously high waves. The fourth man, who is facing the other three, is the only one standing up, and we can't see his face.

I'd always assumed that the painting was simply depicting the literary conflict of man versus nature. For thirty years, I thought it was just a depressing painting, and I had no idea why my grandpa had liked it or bought it. A few years after his death, I asked my grandma if I could have the painting, but not because I liked it. It just reminded me of my grandparents,

151

and I wanted it as a physical, tangible reminder of them and all the good times I had visiting them growing up.

But then a friend came into town to visit me. At that time, I was still coming to grips with my own comprehensive and chronic suffering, feeling abandoned by God and fighting to regain the faith I once held so strongly. As my friend looked at the painting, he drew my attention to things in it that I hadn't noticed. Way off in the distance on the canvas, beyond the storm, is a large ship coming to rescue the men. I couldn't believe that I had never seen it before. I suppose that the large, dark canoe in the middle of the canvas—the present struggle—made other things that were there invisible because I wasn't looking for them. I wasn't expecting anything good. I wasn't anticipating hope or rescue.

Once he pointed that out to me, I started to notice other things I hadn't seen in the painting before. The sky had always just seemed dark, but now I noticed that behind the gray clouds, the artist had painted some blue sky peeking out from a break in the gray cloud cover, and there were even touches of pink. Five white birds were flying overhead. Even the water that was painted in such dark hues in the foreground gave way to lighter, aquamarine-colored water beyond the last big wave the men were seeking to crest. What had always been a despairing and hopeless painting to me became something entirely different: a picture of hope on the horizon despite the chaos of the storm.

In chapter 7, we learned the importance of honest, God-ward lament as we acknowledge the dark clouds and stormy seas in our lives. But in addition to weeping in hurt, we must also practice rejoicing in hope as we live with comprehensive and chronic suffering. In many ways, that journey looks a lot like the scene depicted in the painting. Two seemingly paradoxical concepts coexist as complementary biblical realities. Because the exhausting struggle and the overwhelming storm are real, we weep in hurt. And because sure salvation has come and brighter days are on the horizon, we rejoice in hope.

Though it may seem counterintuitive, lament can lay a foundation for joy, because it allows us to honestly acknowledge that what we're going through is really hard, and it expresses our belief in God's power and goodness and in his plan to redeem what is broken in this life. In that way, honest lament paves the way for an authentic and realistic joy. The Christian worldview is unique in that it neither denies lament nor denies joy. We should be suspicious when believers deny the realities of suffering by hiding their pain or slapping a smile on their faces to give the impression that everything is great. Such a facade is clearly out of touch with the realities of life in a fallen world.

Yet Christians also must not be in a perpetual state of gloom and woe, as though our Lord were still in the grave and all the precious truths of Scripture were not true. As we continue to be sanctified day by day, we grow to be people of both great sorrow and great joy like our Lord Jesus, a "man of sorrows" (Isa. 53:3) who endured suffering "for the joy that was set before him" (Heb. 12:2).

Joy Blockers

Before we consider a few things that can block our joy, a caveat is in order. We all know that joy can seem elusive even under the best of circumstances—how much more so in the face of comprehensive and chronic suffering. So while we are to pursue joy, we must also be careful not to draw rigid conclusions regarding exactly what that joy will look like for everyone.

For example, it's important to remember that we are body-soul beings whose emotional and mental states can be influenced by our physical states. Ask anyone who's ever had the flu and is vomiting, running a fever, and completely drained of energy. We all know that being physically ill puts a damper on our mental faculties and influences our emotional states. Many medical conditions can influence our emotions, including chronic illness, chronic pain, hormone imbalances, thyroid problems, and brain injuries. As a result, we must exercise caution when seeking to assess whether we or others are "joyful *enough*" in any given situation or season of life, for numerous complexities are at play.

Unbelief

While many things may be blocking our experience of joy, two are particularly relevant to our discussion. First and foremost, our experience of joy can be blocked by *unbelief*. Romans 15:13 says, "May the God of hope fill you with all *joy* and peace *in believing*, so that by the power of the Holy Spirit you may abound in hope." Here we see the truth that faith fuels our joy. Many other passages of Scripture note this critical link:

> But I *have trusted* in your steadfast love;
>> my heart *shall rejoice* in your salvation. (Ps. 13:5)

> For you make him most blessed forever;
>> you make him *glad* with the *joy* of your presence.
> For the king *trusts* in the Lord,
>> and through the steadfast love of the Most High he shall
>> not be moved. (Ps. 21:6–7)

> For our heart is *glad* in him,
>> because we *trust* in his holy name. (Ps. 33:21)

> Though you have not seen him, you love him. Though you do not now see him, you *believe* in him and *rejoice* with *joy* that is inexpressible and filled with glory. (1 Peter 1:8)

It's important to note that there's a difference between not "feeling" the reality of the truths of Scripture (but still believing them) and not feeling them while also starting to lose our grip on believing them. That's why chapter 4, which discussed our relationship with God, is the most critical piece of our journey with comprehensive and chronic suffering. If we're doubting that God's Word is true, or maybe thinking that it's true for others but not true for us, then experiencing joy might be virtually impossible because our unbelief is blocking it.

This can be a place where genuine believers find themselves. You may be a "bruised reed" and "a faintly burning wick" (Isa. 42:3; see also Matt. 12:20). When this is the case, what's most important is not your attempts to directly pursue joy, which will likely remain elusive as you struggle against unbelief. What's most important for you in this context is to lay hold of God (as Job did), wrestling with him in prayer and through his Word, as you seek to have your faith strengthened and restored. Faith causes joy to bloom. My encouragement to you if your faith is worn down and turned around by your circumstances is to focus on the fight for your faith and to do so by remaining faithful to reading God's Word and attending corporate worship (if physically possible), reading Christian books that can help you better understand God's character and ways, and receiving counseling from church leaders or a biblical counselor. I know from personal experience how exhausting it is to be in this place, but I can say to you that God is faithful, and though you may have to wait a long time, "everyone who believes in him will not be put to shame" (Rom. 10:11).

Forgetfulness

Even if we are not experiencing these difficulties in our relationship with God, Scripture tells us that forgetting God's work on our behalf can also hinder our joy. Speaking of godly character and living, Peter says, "Whoever lacks these qualities is so *nearsighted* that he is blind, having *forgotten* that he was cleansed from his former sins" (2 Peter 1:9).

Comprehensive and chronic suffering can become so front and center in your life that it becomes difficult to see anything else. The needs of the moment consume you, and you may often feel as though each day is simply a battle to survive on limited resources and energy. You may not have the luxury to thrive; perhaps you're simply trying to stay alive and keep all the spinning plates of your life from crashing to the ground. As a result, daily meditation on and remembrance of the redemptive work of God in your life may get pushed to the periphery. Maybe it seems far away from your daily struggles, even irrelevant.

But the truth is that we need to be reminded of God's work on our behalf, especially when the storms of dark affliction threaten to drag us under the water, disorienting us in a breathless, terrifying tumble in which we struggle to know how to get back to the surface. Far from being mere theological facts, these truths serve as anchors for the soul in the storms (see Heb. 6:19). What is the work that God has accomplished on your behalf, and how can the knowledge of that produce joy in your experience of comprehensive and chronic suffering?

Rejoicing in the Saving Work of God

From start to finish, the story of the Bible is the story of a creator God who pursues and redeems a sinful people for himself through the work of Jesus Christ, so that they might know him and delight in his glory with one another in a perfect world free from sin and suffering for eternity. Such realities were ordained by God before our birth, they inform our present, and they determine our future. Yet today, we find ourselves living in the gap between the unspoiled goodness of Eden in Genesis 1–2 and the consummated perfection of Revelation 21–22. This gap is a place where we experience sin and suffering, and we easily grow weary as we wait for the consummation of all things. But by consciously calling to mind God's saving grace in our lives, we can experience joy as we set these truths in the center of our spiritual sight. What is true of us as Christians? Let's consider how meditating on our deliverance from the darkness of sin and hell can lead to joy. The apostle Paul prays that believers would be

> strengthened with all power, according to his glorious might, for all endurance and patience with *joy*; giving thanks to the Father, who has qualified [us] to share in the inheritance of the saints in light. He has *delivered us from the domain of darkness and transferred us to the kingdom of his beloved Son*. (Col. 1:11–13)

Most of us have heard stories about people in desperate circumstances who despaired of any way out. Perhaps we see on the news the story of a family who is bearing the weight of an exorbitant medical bill they could never pay off, or a hiker who is stranded in a remote location with no ability to communicate with the outside world. These are dire situations that threaten people's very survival. The terror and helplessness in such circumstances would be palpable. And deliverance from these situations—whether it be a medical bill canceled or paid for by an outside party, or a rescue team finding the stranded hiker—would likewise bring a level of relief and joy that could not be contained or surpassed.

As dire as these examples are, they pale in comparison to the plight of hell-bound sinners such as we were. We desperately needed our enormous spiritual debt to be paid, and we desperately needed to be rescued from the worst of all possible destinations. In Christ, God has not only rescued us from the domain of darkness but also brought us into his eternal kingdom of light.

Speaking of this redemptive work, the apostle Paul notes,

> But when the fullness of time had come, God sent forth his Son, born of woman, born under the law, to redeem those who were under the law, so that we might receive *adoption as sons*. . . . So you are no longer a slave, but a son, and if a son, then an heir through God. (Gal. 4:4–5, 7)

Not only does the perfect life and substitutionary death of Christ secure rescue from hell for those who place their faith in him; it also changes the status of our relationship with God. Once his enemies because of our sinful rebellion, we become his beloved children through our union with Christ. God is no longer against us but incontrovertibly *for* us (see Ps. 56:9). And because we are his children, we are "heirs of God and fellow heirs with Christ" (Rom. 8:17). Some of us may receive an earthly inheritance from family members in this life; others may not. Yet even the most lavish earthly inheritance one could receive from the wealthiest individual on earth is nothing compared to the matchless gift of being heirs of God and fellow heirs with Christ.

As we've discussed throughout this book, it certainly may not *feel* as though you are a child and an heir of the King of the universe in your comprehensive and chronic suffering. You may wonder, Does my suffering perhaps mean that I'm not the child and heir I thought I was? It's almost as though Paul anticipated this question. He immediately goes on to say, "provided we suffer with him in order that we may also be glorified with him" (v. 17). The shape of the life of our Lord shows us that suffering precedes glory. Therefore, don't be surprised when you travel the same trajectory, interpreting your suffering not as a sign of his displeasure or abandonment but as a sign that you are following Jesus, who "for the joy that was set before him endured the cross, despising the shame, and is seated at the right hand of the throne of God" (Heb. 12:2).

Rejoicing in the Creational Works of God

While the blessings of God's saving work in our lives form the foundation of our joy, these truths can sometimes be difficult to wholeheartedly and confidently believe when we're experiencing comprehensive and chronic suffering that challenges our faith and our relationship with God. When you're walking through the difficult process of seeking to develop a deeper knowledge of God that can coexist with inexplicable suffering and loss, most of your time and attention will be directed toward a restored relationship with him, and the pursuit of joy in biblical truths you're struggling to grasp may feel forced or artificial. Sometimes, it may even make you feel worse (see Ps. 77:3).

If you are in that place, a more accessible way to experience joy in the glory and goodness of God is by delighting in his creative works on display in the world. Scripture repeatedly points to God's glory being manifested in creation and the joy that results from beholding his works. For example, Psalm 19:1–2 says,

> The heavens declare the glory of God,
>> and the sky above proclaims his handiwork.
> Day to day pours out speech,
>> and night to night reveals knowledge.

These glorious works of God are many: "O Lord, how manifold are your works! In wisdom have you made them all; the earth is full of your creatures" (Ps. 104:24). The psalmist goes on to say, "May the glory of the Lord endure forever; may the Lord rejoice in his works" (v. 31).

Beholding God's attributes through his creation leads the believer to delight: "You, O Lord, have made me glad by your work; at the works of your hands I sing for joy" (Ps. 92:4). Thus, we can cultivate joy—even amid sorrow—by intentionally turning our gaze to the heavens above and to the earth below as we behold God's glory through the things that he has made, even if it's in seemingly small ways. For me, it was certainly easier and more soul-satisfying to rejoice in God's works when I was surrounded by the natural beauty of towering mountains and roaring oceans in California. I found it difficult to behold the beauty of nature after moving to a flat, landlocked Texas city surrounded by concrete, strip malls, brown houses, brown fences, and brown grass.

But difficult circumstances and surroundings require us to be joy-hunters who are willing to search for beauty in small ways and in unexpected places—all the while knowing that one day, we will be surrounded by unimaginable splendor for all eternity. But today, we rejoice in the little things—the branches of a tree swaying in the wind, birds calling to one another, ants marching across the ground, a beautiful sunset, a thundering storm—and we praise the God who created such a magnificent earth.

But there's much more to rejoice in than simply nature. Paul instructs the Corinthians, "Whether you eat or drink, or whatever you do, do all to the glory of God" (1 Cor. 10:31). We can experience joy and glorify God in the seemingly mundane things of life, all the way down to food and drink. Paul expands this truth further in his letter to Timothy, where he says,

> For everything created by God is good, and nothing is to be rejected if it is received with thanksgiving, for it is made holy by the word of God and prayer. (1 Tim. 4:4–5)

Comprehensive and chronic suffering takes so much of the "normal" out of life and the things that people typically rejoice in. But if we're willing to take pleasure in the small things, we'll find that there is still pleasure to be had and gifts of God to be recognized and enjoyed. We can watch things that make us laugh, remembering that God is the one who created us with the capacity for humor, and thank him for the gift of laughter. We can listen to beautiful music and sing, remembering that God is the one who enables all artistic ability and who created our ears to perceive pleasing sounds. Even if we have dietary restrictions or financial limitations, every once in a while, we can eat a small treat, remembering that God is the one who created our tongues to have taste buds so that we could experience pleasure from food and drink.

Or perhaps we can dance, play an instrument, draw, write, or engage in other hobbies or artistic endeavors, even if they're on a very small scale or even if they're only something that we're able to do occasionally.

Comprehensive and chronic suffering is deeply draining. But if you are willing to embrace small things, it is possible for you to experience little joys, and in so doing, you remember the God who created a world for you to enjoy and who created you with the capacity to enjoy it. And perhaps in these ways, you'll be brought closer once again to a true understanding of who God is and experience some measure of restoration with him, even as you wrestle through hard questions and may still feel some distance from him.

The God Who Rejoices Over Us

As we've seen, we can experience joy as we meditate on God's saving work in our salvation and behold his works in creation. But there's a third way that we can experience joy in God, and it's perhaps the most stunning of all. It is the truth that the holy, sovereign, infinite God himself rejoices over *us*. If you are a believer in Christ, your God rejoices over *you*.

The prophet Isaiah says this to the people of Israel:

> You shall no more be termed Forsaken,
>> and your land shall no more be termed Desolate,
>
> but you shall be called *My Delight Is in Her*,
>> and your land Married;
>
> *for the Lord delights in you,*
>> and your land shall be married.
>
> For as a young man marries a young woman,
>> so shall your sons marry you,
>
> and as the bridegroom rejoices over the bride,
>> *so shall your God rejoice over you.* (Isa. 62:4–5)

We, like Israel, were forsaken and desolate because of our sin. But through the grace of God in the redeeming work of Christ, we are not simply declared righteous before God, and he does not merely tolerate us. Rather, God delights in us as a groom rejoices in his bride. It's difficult to think of a more powerful comparison than the one Isaiah draws here.

I've heard it said by multiple people that when they attend a wedding, instead of watching the bride as she walks down the aisle, they watch the groom's face as he beholds his bride walking toward him. The unbridled joy that the groom feels as he sees his bride is but a faint echo of the superior joy that the Lord has in his own. While this may be hard for you to believe for any number of reasons, it is what the Bible declares to be truth, and the more you meditate on and believe this truth, the greater your own experience of joy will be.

The prophet Zephaniah voices this same truth when he declares, "The Lord your God is in your midst, a mighty one who will save; *he will rejoice over you with gladness,* he will quiet you by his love; *he will exult over you with loud singing*" (Zeph. 3:17). God, who is infinitely powerful as a warrior, is at the same time the one who rejoices over you with gladness. This imagery conveys wholehearted happiness and fullness of joy that overflows to the point of loud singing.

Though we cannot yet see him with our physical eyes and cannot yet hear him with our physical ears, we can lay hold of these truths by faith, and as we do, we'll experience his joy.

Micro-Futures and Macro-Futures

There's something about the stillness and quietness of night as we lie in bed waiting to fall asleep. Of course, troubled thoughts about the future can strike at any time of day. But those moments between wakeful activity and oblivious slumber can be an especially potent time when fearful thoughts arise.

When we fret about our own futures, what we're really thinking about is what we might call our "micro-futures." We're thinking about what may or may not happen to us in the next two years, five years, ten years, twenty years, or even fifty years. Perhaps you lie awake at night wondering how your medical condition may worsen, or how your money may run out, or who will be there to take care of you. Our prospects may be terrifying, and we can easily become untethered as we instinctively master the unhelpful art of catastrophizing about our micro-futures.

But the truth is, no matter how much time we spend spinning our wheels and wondering how things will play out in the years to come, we simply have no idea what will happen to us. Not only that, but we don't even have much control over these things anyway.

Yet while our micro-futures certainly matter, we must also learn the art of meditating on our macro-futures, which leads to joy. We can't answer any of the questions about our micro-futures, but God's Word gives us ample material for hope-filled meditation as we consider our macro-futures. Five, ten, twenty, even fifty years seems like a very long time when we think about the future of our earthly lives. But even one hundred years is nothing more than a single drop in the roaring ocean of eternity. As some have said, if eternity is like an unending line, our lives here and now are like a tiny dot on that line. The dot certainly matters for eternity, as we discussed in chapter 6, but when it comes to fortifying our souls, meditation on our eternal and sure macro-futures can bring comfort, joy, and peace that are impossible to obtain when we merely consider our micro-futures.

In 2 Corinthians 4:18, the apostle Paul says, "We look not to the things that are seen but to the things that are unseen. For the things that are seen are transient, but the things that are unseen are eternal." What are the sure but unseen things that lay ahead for us as God's children? Let's turn to consider some of them now, using Revelation 21 and 22 as our guide.

We Will See God

The greatest future hope we have as believers is what theologians call the "beatific vision." This is the fulfillment of the promise that we will see God face-to-face when we shed this mortal body. And it's nothing new—God's people have longed to behold him throughout the ages. Amid his misery, Job declared,

I know that my Redeemer lives,
  and at the last he will stand upon the earth.
And after my skin has been thus destroyed,
  yet in my flesh I shall see God,
whom I shall see for myself,
  and my eyes shall behold, and not another. (Job
    19:25–27)

Moses prayed to the Lord, "Show me your glory" (Ex. 33:18). And our Lord Jesus, who makes visible the invisible God, told us, "Blessed are the pure in heart, for they shall see God" (Matt. 5:8).

These longings and promises come to fruition in Revelation 22:4, which says that God's people "will see his face." This vision of God is not physical, for neither the Father nor the Spirit have bodies. Yet in a way we cannot now understand, we will "see" and experience the glory of God in ways that exceed our greatest imaginings. Not only that, but we will one day physically behold the ascended Jesus in his glorified body.

If you think back to the happiest day you've ever experienced and how that made you feel, beholding the glory of God unhindered by your sin and suffering will radically and eternally surpass that day. It's hard to conceive of this level of blessedness. But meditating on this truth and fixing your hope on this promise can fill your heart with joy even now.

God Will Dwell with Us

Not only will we see God, but we will dwell with him forever. When we trace the redemptive storyline of the Old Testament, we see the theme of God's dwelling with his people signified in various ways. In the garden of Eden, Adam and Eve enjoyed fellowship with the Lord before their fall into sin (see Gen. 3:8). Despite the sin of mankind, God revealed his desire and commitment to dwell among a people he calls to himself: "Let them make me a sanctuary, that I may dwell in their midst" (Ex. 25:8). When God rescued his people out of Egypt, he dwelt with them in the wilderness through the tabernacle, a tent that both protected the people from his holiness and provided a way for them to approach him (see Ex. 40:34–35). This temporary structure later gave way to the temple in Jerusalem. But both the tabernacle and the temple pointed to a greater reality to come: the Son of God incarnate, who would dwell (literally, "tabernacle") among us (see John 1:14).

The psalmists express their longing to be in God's presence, echoing the hearts of God's people through the ages.

I shall dwell in the house of the Lord forever. (Ps. 23:6)

One thing have I asked of the Lord,
    that will I seek after:
that I may dwell in the house of the Lord
    all the days of my life,
to gaze upon the beauty of the Lord
    and to inquire in his temple. (Ps. 27:4)

How lovely is your dwelling place,
    O Lord of hosts!
My soul longs, yes, faints
    for the courts of the Lord;

> my heart and flesh sing for joy
>> to the living God. (Ps. 84:1–2)

> Blessed are those who dwell in your house,
>> ever singing your praise! (Ps. 84:4)

By virtue of Christ's redemptive work, God dwells with us now through the Holy Spirit (see John 14:16–17). Though we have been reconciled to God, sin still hinders a perfect experience of this restored relationship. We don't yet see God in his full glory, our affections for him are often weak, and, as Paul says, "we see in a mirror dimly" (1 Cor. 13:12). But Revelation 21:3 shows us the consummation of this theme of God's dwelling with us: "Behold, the dwelling place of God is with man. He will dwell with them, and they will be his people, and God himself will be with them as their God." All your longings to be near the Lord will be met, and you will be together forever with the triune God who has purchased you and made you his own, that you might behold his glory and dwell with him for eternity. This thought fuels unspeakable joy (see 1 Peter 1:8).

The Former Things Will Pass Away

Not only will we see God and dwell with him forever, but our lives in eternity will be devoid of all the trials, hardships, inconveniences, and heartaches of this fallen world: "[God] will wipe away every tear from [our] eyes, and death shall be no more, neither shall there be mourning, nor crying, nor pain anymore, for the former things have passed away" (Rev. 21:4).

We are so accustomed to living in a fallen world that it's hard to conceive of a life unmarred by sin and suffering. So many things that we need now will be unnecessary in the world to come. This reality hit home to me when I was at a drugstore filling a prescription. As I waited, I noticed the layout of the store. Giant signs hung from the ceiling over each aisle, telling shoppers where to find what they needed: antacids, hearing aids, crutches, vitamins, bandages, blood pressure medicine, and on and on. It struck me that such stores wouldn't exist apart from the fall. God created a world in which we didn't need drugstores, and we turned it into one where we do.

But Jesus is coming. And he will "'shake not only the earth but also the heavens' . . . in order that the things that cannot be shaken may remain" (Heb. 12:26–27). Sin and suffering will be shaken out; righteousness and shalom will remain. Rejecters of God will be shaken out; believers in Jesus Christ will remain. King Jesus will reign, and we will have glorified bodies on a new earth in which we won't be able to find a drugstore anywhere, because, gloriously, we won't need one anymore. The things that we now must exert so much time, energy, and effort trying to reverse, ameliorate, or maintain will no longer be needed.

What will it be like for us to instantly go from a world filled with groaning to a world filled with glory? In February 2021, Texas experienced a severe weather event known as "The Great Texas Freeze." Temperatures plunged below 0 degrees Fahrenheit. Millions lost power and were unable to heat their homes. Water pipes froze and burst, destroying houses. There was a major freeway accident that involved a pileup of over a hundred vehicles. During this weeklong event, hundreds died and billions of dollars' worth of property damage took place. It was a scary time. But the strangest part of the whole ordeal was how quickly everything changed. Once the sun came out again, the havoc wreaked by the cold and ice literally melted under its heat. A walk in the neighborhood that two days before could have landed me in the emergency room with an injury turned into a joyful, victorious stroll as I trampled over slushy piles of water. The dangerous ice melted, turning into harmless water, and everything that had been so threatening and sinister evaporated.

So it is with this world. Everything bad that we face today will one day be "former things." Sin and suffering will be forever banished, and all their tragedy and treachery will melt before the blazing glory of the Son, who will conquer all his foes and ours, and whose kingdom shall know no end.

New Things Will Come

Having been cleansed from all sin and freed from all suffering, our future life will be an eternal reign of righteousness and shalom. Jesus promises us, "Behold, I am making all things new" (Rev. 21:5). In this new world, we will rule and reign with Christ, not in the sense that we will be equal to him but in the sense that our original mandate in the garden of Eden to rule and subdue the earth will be fully restored (see Gen. 1:26–31). Under the authority of our sovereign God, we will even judge fallen angels at the end of the age (see 1 Cor. 6:3). God promises us that "if we endure, we will also reign with him" (2 Tim. 2:12). It's hard to understand why God would want to give us any rulership or authority at all, but in his lavish grace, he will, and "the Lord God will be [our] light, and [we] will reign forever and ever" (Rev. 22:5).

Do you feel like a future king or queen right now in your comprehensive and chronic suffering? Probably not. If anything, life may feel more like an action movie where the president's child gets taken hostage and held for ransom by nefarious agents. We long for our Father, we long for our true home, and we long to be everything that God intended for us to be when he created humankind. But in Jesus Christ, our ransom has already been paid, and he is returning to slay the wicked, end our suffering, and take us home to be with him.

Horror will give way to honor, groaning will give way to glory, and heartache will give way to happiness—forever.

CONCLUSION

As I write this conclusion, it is a dark and dreary day outside. There's a damp chill in the air, the kind that makes you feel cold on the inside, unable to warm up. The gray sky casts a deathlike pallor over everything. The cloud cover feels suffocating, making it impossible to see the sky that declares God's glory and proclaims his handiwork (see Ps. 19:1). And the sun—what sun? It seems to have been completely snuffed out. One cannot feel its warmth or see its rays reflecting and creating brilliance in the world.

Our journey heavenward can sometimes feel similar when we are experiencing comprehensive and chronic suffering. The light seems to have been extinguished; the darkness seems to prevail. Limping our way through deep valleys and over towering mountains is arduous. We are tempted to give up. We wonder if we will ever see or feel the sun again. We fear our faith might fail.

Yet we press on, for the heavenly city awaits us. The laborious terrain will eventually lead us to a broad vista—to the place where God dwells and where we will dwell with him. And though we may feel alone in our journey, God promises that we are not, for he is with us (see Pss. 23:4; 139:7–12), preserving our souls and empowering us to hold fast to him in saving faith.

Thus, let us continue limping heavenward with this rallying cry:

> The hill, though high, I covet to ascend,
> The difficulty will not me offend;
> For I perceive the way to life lies here.
> Come, pluck up, Heart, let's neither faint nor fear.[1]

Appendix

HOW TO HELP THOSE WHO FACE COMPREHENSIVE AND CHRONIC SUFFERING

"Miserable comforters are you all." This was Job's assessment of the three friends who came to be with him in his suffering (Job 16:2). None of us want to be miserable comforters to those who are suffering. Yet all of us can too easily assume that *we* aren't the miserable comforters. It's *other* people who need instruction, guidance, and sometimes even rebuke for how they speak to and treat those who are suffering.

But we must be humble enough to realize that as much as we'd like to think we could never be miserable comforters, we likely have been at some point. Therefore, it behooves us to learn how we can provide Christlike care to those around us who are hurting as we grow in obedience to our Lord's command:

A new commandment I give to you, that you love one another: just as I have loved you, you also are to love one another. By this all people will know that you are my disciples, if you have love for one another. (John 13:34–35)

Much more could be said about how to walk alongside those experiencing comprehensive and chronic suffering, but the seven guidelines outlined below can provide a helpful framework for both individuals and churches who are seeking to care well for those facing deep and painful affliction. It may also be helpful to reread chapter 2, which discussed five ways that people may respond poorly to sufferers (through accusations, aphorisms, abandonment, avoidance, and apathy).

One final note before we begin: As you review the material in chapter 2 and the seven guidelines below, you may want to note any thoughts or emotions that you experience as you read. Sometimes we fail to come alongside sufferers because of our own incorrect theology or deep-seated fears. Addressing these things can better position you to love others well and can foster growth and maturity in your own life as you follow Christ.

Lament with Them

In Romans 12:15, the apostle Paul writes, "Rejoice with those who rejoice, weep with those who weep." Unfortunately, when people interact with sufferers, they often (whether intentionally or unintentionally) switch around the words in these verses. As a result, they attempt to "rejoice with those who weep." But Proverbs warns us that "whoever sings songs to a heavy heart is like one who takes off a garment on a cold day, and like vinegar on soda" (Prov. 25:20).

There are many reasons why we might be tempted to take this approach with a sufferer. Perhaps we think that the saying "laugher is the best medicine" applies to all people, at all times, in all circumstances. Perhaps we're uncomfortable with expressions of grief, both in our own lives and with others, and are doing whatever we can to avoid that experience. Perhaps we feel like our "job" with a sufferer is to somehow artificially and prematurely force them to feel better as soon as possible. The problem is, this doesn't help sufferers who need to grieve and lament the brokenness they are experiencing.

Tension and dissonance arise in the souls of sufferers when their grief is bottled up inside and needs to be expressed, yet the people around them refuse to acknowledge or enter into their grief with them. And when sufferers can't healthily grieve before the Lord and with his people, they can get overwhelmed with turbulent emotions that remain unexpressed. There is "a time to weep" (Eccl. 3:4), and we need not be afraid to enter into such grief with others.

If we desire to show Christlike care for sufferers, we must be willing to, in a sense, descend into the pit with them. This requires a willing choice on our part because sometimes we avoid entering into the deep and dark suffering of others— afraid that we will not know what to say or do, or afraid of entering into the emotional intensity of another's griefs and pains. But when it comes to our brothers and sisters in Christ who are suffering, avoiding or refusing to step into the suffering with them is not an option, because it is not the way of Christ. Jesus easily could have run from suffering and death, but he did the opposite. He ran toward it as he "set his face to go to Jerusalem" (Luke 9:51), where he would be betrayed, mocked, condemned, and murdered—all for the sake of those whom he came to save. Therefore, we model Christ and embody his care for his people when we, too, resolutely determine to face difficult things by entering into others' pain.

In other words, growing in Christlikeness means following in the footsteps of Jesus, whose love for others always came at a cost to himself. Let us then seek to step into the shoes of those who are suffering. Let us sit down next to them on the ash heap of their lives, listening to them until we are emotionally moved by what they have faced and are facing in their lives. Let us be sad with them and weep with them, lamenting the things that *should be* that *are not* and the things that *are* that *should not be.* Let us acknowledge with them that the world is broken and mourn that reality together as we await the triumphant return of our Lord Jesus.

Be Angry on Their Behalf

Closely related to weeping with those who weep is being angry on the behalf of those who are suffering. At first glance, this may seem strange or even wrong. After all, isn't anger a sin? And wouldn't our expression of anger only make their suffering worse or tempt them to sin? While there are times when our anger is sinful and unredemptive, this is not always the case.

Author Kelly Kapic helpfully describes the kind of anger that helps sufferers:

> If I am really upset about something, my wife hears about it, and then she enters into my frustrations and voices similar concern, a funny thing often happens: I calm down. I don't have to keep being so angry, because now I can see that someone else feels my pain, believes my frustration, and

senses that something has gone wrong. . . . What I need is not for someone to tell me everything is okay; I need them to acknowledge that something is wrong—that I am not insane, but a real problem is at hand. When I see that others believe this, know this, feel this, I can calm down. I have received a witness.[1]

We see this display of righteous anger in our Lord Jesus during his earthly life in a sinful and suffering world. In "The Emotional Life of Our Lord," theologian B. B. Warfield writes of the indignation that Jesus expressed throughout the Gospels. He notes, "It would be impossible . . . for a moral being to stand in the presence of perceived wrong indifferent and unmoved. Precisely what we mean by a moral being is a being perceptive of the difference between right and wrong and reacting appropriately to right and wrong perceived as such. The emotions of indignation and anger belong therefore to the very self-expression of a moral being as such and cannot be lacking to him in the presence of wrong."[2]

Warfield then comments on the scene of Jesus at Lazarus's tomb, in which the text tells us that Jesus "was deeply moved in his spirit and greatly troubled" (John 11:33). He notes that Jesus's state here was not that of "uncontrollable grief, but of irrepressible anger,"[3] and that "the spectacle of the distress of Mary and her companions enraged Jesus because it brought poignantly home to his consciousness the evil of death, its unnaturalness, its 'violent tyranny.'"[4] He goes on to say that Jesus's "anger is not merely the seamy side of his pity; it is the righteous reaction of his moral sense in the presence of evil. But Jesus burned with anger against the wrongs he met with in his journey through human life as truly as he melted with pity at the sight of the world's misery: and it was out of these two emotions that his actual mercy proceeded."[5]

Being angry about the afflictions that others endure can be a Christlike expression of care that accurately responds to the realities of life in a fallen world. While Jesus did speak to Lazarus's sister Martha about resurrection hope, his response to the situation was not simply to tell everyone gathered to keep their chins up and rejoice about the future resurrection. Rather, Jesus wept, and Jesus got angry. Angry at the destruction, loss, lack of flourishing, and separation that death in all its forms produces. And his anger, combined with his compassion, propelled him forward to accomplish the will of God and sacrificially love those for whom he would die.

Christ's call to us as his people is to love those who suffer with this same love. And this love includes anger at how sin, in all its expressions in a fallen world, hurts people created in God's image. We should be angry at how sin brings suffering into people's lives. We should allow our anger to proclaim the truth rather than to cover over it or minimize it. By bearing witness with sufferers through our anger, we agree with them—and with our God—that the world is not yet as it should be and that wrongs have yet to be righted.

Focus on What You Have in Common, Not What Separates You

By its very nature, comprehensive and chronic suffering is isolating in many respects—relationally, physically, emotionally, and geographically. People who suffer in these ways are often disconnected from what is perceived as "normal" life by other Christians, and their lives aren't characterized by the same rhythms, opportunities, advantages, and experiences as the "average" person or family.

While it's understandable that conversation in church small groups, Bible studies, or other social gatherings will involve the temporal things of everyday life, talking exclusively or primarily about temporal things often alienates sufferers living what we'd consider an "abnormal" life, making them unable to participate in the conversations happening around them.

Such experiences can be discouraging enough in sufferers' interactions with unbelievers. But when activities and gatherings within the body of Christ that are supposed to center on what we have in common—being united to God and to one another through our Lord Jesus Christ, growing in his Word, pursuing him and his kingdom, and living for him—instead revolve around the same things that unbelievers place their focus on, sufferers do not receive the strength and encouragement that they desperately need. Even worse, they may come away from such interactions with a heavier weight of discouragement and sorrow than they arrived with. Why? Because they wanted to connect with other believers on the things that they have in common, but instead they were reminded of how different and abnormal their lives seem compared to the lives of Christians around them.

The writer of Hebrews exhorted his hearers not to "[neglect] to meet together, as is the habit of some, but [to encourage] one another, and all the more as you see the Day drawing near" (Heb. 10:25). This is a call for us not only to remain vitally connected to a body of believers through the local church but also to use that time together to build up, strengthen, and encourage one another in the race of faith. That's not to say that we can't enjoy casual conversations and leisure activities together in the body of Christ. We can and should do such things. But it's also a reminder that the Christian life is difficult, that we wrestle against spiritual forces of evil (see Eph. 6:12), and that our primary goal as Christians is to help one another remain faithful to our Lord in this life.

As we seek to love those who are living with comprehensive and chronic suffering, we should be aware of and sensitive to these realities. We must remember who we are with and seek to understand what they are facing, and we should endeavor to interact in ways that are the most encouraging to the people around us rather than defaulting to conversational autopilot. In so doing, we seek to imitate Jesus, who knew "how to sustain with a word him who is weary" (Isa. 50:4). "A bruised reed he will not break, and a faintly burning wick he will not quench" (Isa. 42:3).

Don't Just Pray for Them: Be the Answer to Their Prayers When You Can

James, the half brother of Jesus, writes in his epistle,

If a brother or sister is poorly clothed and lacking in daily food, and one of you says to them, "Go in peace, be warmed and filled," without giving them the things needed for the body, what good is that? (James 2:15–16)

The answer, of course, is "Not much." In context, James is referring to people who claim to have faith but whose lives are not characterized by the good works that true faith produces. In a broader sense, his words point out our tendency to do what is easy and convenient (pronouncing a benediction on someone in need) rather than actually working to meet the needs of that person.

It's a wonderful thing to pray for people. Prayer can be an expression of love, care, and sacrifice as we bring a person's needs before the Lord and ask him to strengthen, bless, and provide for them. But sometimes, prayer can serve as an easy way to feel like we're helping someone more than we actually are. We take a few seconds to pray for someone, and then we continue with our day.

To counter this tendency, we must honestly consider how we might not only pray but also be the means that God uses to answer those prayers. James might say it this way: "If a brother or sister is unemployed and financially struggling, and one of you says to them, 'I'll be praying for you,' but doesn't help with their financial need or assist them in finding a job, what good is that?" Or he might say, "If a brother or sister is isolated and lonely, and one of you says to them, 'I'll be praying for you,' but doesn't call them, visit them, or invite them over, what good is that?"

Let's not use prayer to simply mark off a mental checkbox to convince ourselves that we've helped someone. Prayer is a wonderful thing to bring before the Lord on behalf of our brothers and sisters in Christ. But, as we'll see next, we need to be willing to do more than pray when we're able to.

Realize That True Compassion Leads to Action

It is easy to feel sorrow or compassion for a person's difficult circumstances and to convince ourselves that we've actually helped that person because of our emotional response—but we haven't. The emotion of compassion is meant to propel us forward into action on another person's behalf. We see this pattern consistently in the ministry of Jesus as recorded in the Gospels. Compassion leads to action.

Jesus's compassion-fueled action stands in stark contrast to apathy, which he illustrated most graphically in the parable of the good Samaritan (see Luke 10:25–37). Stripped and beaten by robbers, a man lay alongside the road, where a priest and a Levite saw him and passed by on the other side. This parable should shock us. It wasn't that the Jewish priest and the Jewish Levite didn't see this presumably Jewish man lying bloodied and beaten up on the ground. They saw him, and they walked on by, leaving him for dead. By contrast, a Samaritan—who would have been despised by the Jewish people—saw him and had compassion.

Yet if compassion meant nothing more than feeling bad for the man and offering up a quick prayer that God would help him, then this Samaritan would have been no different from the priest or the Levite. Jesus goes on to explain the tangible fruit of the Samaritan's compassion:

> He went to him and bound up his wounds, pouring on oil and wine. Then he set him on his own animal and brought him to an inn and took care of him. And the next day he took out two denarii and gave them to the innkeeper, saying, "Take care of him, and whatever more you spend, I will repay you when I come back." (10:34–35)

Compassion led him to take powerful action on the beaten man's behalf: binding up his wounds, bringing him to an inn, paying for his room, taking care of him, and vowing to return to check on him and pay any outstanding debts. The priest and the Levite, who would have been considered the most "spiritual," the most "godly," and the most "mature" to Jesus's listeners, willfully walked by a brother in need and left him for dead. It was the despised Samaritan who exemplified what true love for God and neighbor looked like.

Jesus says in Matthew 25:40, "Truly, I say to you, as you did it to one of the least of these my brothers, you did it to me." Our compassionate action on behalf of others—which usually requires courage, humility, and sacrifice on our part—can result in a beautiful display of the union that believers share with Christ and with one another. When we see another human being in need, we see our Lord Jesus Christ himself and either help or don't help him as we help or don't help that individual.

Understand the Difference Between Scripture's Comfort and Scripture's Call

One way to categorize what we read in the Bible is to distinguish between the comfort of Scripture and the call of Scripture. Or, to put it more technically, to distinguish between *indicatives* and *imperatives*. The indicatives in Scripture are all of God's promises to us as well as the grace we have received through our union with Christ and our covenant relationship with the triune God. The indicatives not only educate us about who God is and what he has done for us; they also bring us comfort, stability, assurance, joy, encouragement, and strength. Scripture's imperatives, on the other hand, are the call we have as new creations in Christ who are indwelt by the Spirit and who live out that covenant relationship to God as we ever grow in love for both him and others.

Miserable comforters often instinctively and exclusively issue the call of the imperatives to suffering people rather than the comfort of the indicatives. In other words, a miserable comforter consistently leads with questions such as "What do you have to be thankful for right now?" or "How can you rejoice in your circumstances right now?" or "How do you think God wants you to grow and change?" Of course, there may come legitimate times to ask questions like these, especially if the sufferer is guilty of blatant, unrepentant sin. But when people are experiencing comprehensive and chronic suffering, it is far more likely that what they need most is our active presence as loving friends and the strengthening encouragement that comes when we remind them of the indicatives of Scripture—especially when dark suffering clouds the care and presence of God from their perception and experience.

What does focusing on comfort look like as we love sufferers? As we've already noted, it looks like grieving and lamenting with them over their lives and circumstances. It looks like expressing godly anger and indignation at the evil and suffering they've faced and are facing. It looks like providing practical help. In short, it looks like helping them see the loving heart of God toward them (which they may not sense at all) by offering our loving emotions, words, and actions (which they *will* find more tangible).

Be Sensitive to Seasons

The author of Ecclesiastes tells us this: "For everything there is a season, and a time for every matter under heaven"

(3:1). God has structured his world in a particular way, and so we must be sensitive to the fact that different seasons naturally call for different responses. At times, we may be tempted to treat all circumstances and seasons exactly the same—which ultimately leads us to respond to sufferers poorly.

Proverbs 15:23 says, "To make an apt answer is a joy to a man, and a word in season, how good it is!" A word in season is good; it blesses the one to whom it is spoken. But a word "out of season" harms the one to whom it is spoken. Growing in Christ, who is himself the wisdom of God, means that we will grow in wisdom as well, and one way we grow in wisdom is to learn to correctly assess the season (or context) of our words in addition to the words themselves (the content). Context matters.

Remember Solomon's wisdom: "Whoever sings songs to a heavy heart is like one who takes off a garment on a cold day, and like vinegar on soda" (Prov. 25:20). But the question is, how do we know what a sufferer needs most at any given moment? How do we know whether their heavy heart will be blessed by our lament or will be blessed by a little laughter and levity? One mistake we might make while seeking to help sufferers is to think that God and others expect us to be mind readers. We might think that Christian maturity means being able to instinctively intuit what another person needs at any given moment. But that's a heavy (and often impossible) burden for a human being to bear.

If we feel this burden of omniscience, we may be so unsure of what to do or say that we become paralyzed and withdraw from the suffering person without doing or saying anything. Other times, we might ignorantly move toward the suffering person, assuming that what we would personally find helpful is the same thing that the sufferer will find helpful. We then do or say that thing, and it ends up either not helping the sufferer at all or perhaps even hurting them more.

Is this a no-win situation? Should we just give up on even trying to help a suffering person? Not at all. We simply need to recognize that God and others aren't placing upon us the burden of omniscience. Sometimes we might know what is helpful for a specific person, but most times we just aren't sure what they really need. The good news is that the solution doesn't require reading countless books or spending countless hours trying to figure out how best to help someone. The simple solution is this: Ask the suffering person what would be most helpful to them in that moment. Try asking questions like these: "Do you need laughter or lament right now?" or "What would be most helpful to you right now?"

We must also recognize that suffering people are on a journey with the Lord through deep and dark valleys. They are likely being forced to confront biblical truths in new ways that may take them a lot of time to integrate into their lives. They are engaged in the often-long process of trying to reconcile familiar, once-embraced truths with a horrendous experience of ongoing suffering. As they do so, they are working to develop a more comprehensive and robust understanding of God's character and ways. So be patient with them as the Lord is patient with you.

Conclusion

Christians are members of one body. When one member suffers, the other members should seek to relieve that suffering. In so doing, we love the sufferer, and we love God as we love him through the sufferer. As we seek to bear witness and bear burdens with them, we love them by lamenting with them, being angry on their behalf, focusing on what we have in common, helping to answer their prayers, allowing our compassion to propel us forward into practical action, understanding the difference between Scripture's call and Scripture's comfort, and being sensitive to changing seasons. This ministry should be taking place not only through one-on-one relationships but also through the local church as pastors, elders, and deacons care for the flock that God has entrusted to them.

NOTES

Chapter 1: Orienting Ourselves

1   R.C. Sproul, *Surprised by Suffering: The Role of Pain and Death in the Christian Life* (Reformation Trust Publishing, 2010), 1.

2   Paul David Tripp, *Suffering: Gospel Hope When Life Doesn't Make Sense* (Crossway, 2018), 46.

3   Darby Strickland, *Trauma: Caring for Survivors* (P&R Publishing, 2023), 3.

Chapter 2: Miserable Comforters

1   Zack Eswine, *Recovering Eden: The Gospel According to Ecclesiastes* (P&R Publishing, 2014), 122.

2   Eswine, 123.

Chapter 3: The Ancient Serpent

1   Sam Benstead and Gareth Johnson, dirs., *The Puppet Master: Hunting the Ultimate Conman* (Netflix, 2022).

2   Paul David Tripp, *Suffering: Gospel Hope When Life Doesn't Make Sense* (Crossway, 2018), 94.

3   Tripp, 156.

4   Christopher Ash, *Job: The Wisdom of the Cross*, Preaching the Word (Crossway, 2014), 427.

Chapter 4: The God Who Is

1   Notes on "The Book of Job," in *Reformation Study Bible*, ed. R.C. Sproul (Reformation Trust Publishing, 2015).

2   W. Robert Godfrey, *Learning to Love the Psalms* (Reformation Trust Publishing, 2017), 154.

3   Commentary on Isaiah 63:9, in Matthew Henry, *Commentary on the Whole Bible*. Available online at https://www.ccel.org/h/henry/mhc2/.

4   Christopher Ash, *Job: The Wisdom of the Cross*, Preaching the Word (Crossway, 2014), 140.

5   Ash, 213.

6   Commentary on Psalm 56:8, in Henry, *Commentary*.

7   Note on Job 40:15–24, in *Reformation Study Bible*.

8   Note on Job 41:34, in *Reformation Study Bible*.

9   Notes on "The Book of Job," in *Reformation Study Bible*.

10   Ash, *Job*, 191–92.

11   Kelly M. Kapic, *Embodied Hope: A Theological Meditation on Pain and Suffering* (IVP Academic, 2017), 81, referencing John 10:25–38.

Chapter 5: How God Treats His Friends

1   Notes on "The Book of Jeremiah," in *Reformation Study Bible*, ed. R.C. Sproul (Reformation Trust Publishing, 2015).

2   Notes on "Introduction to Jeremiah," in *ESV Study Bible*, eds. Lane T. Dennis and Wayne Grudem (Crossway, 2008).

3   Note on Matthew 11:3–5, in *ESV Study Bible*.

4   Note on Matthew 11:2, in *Reformation Study Bible*.

5   Dan G. McCartney, *Why Does It Have to Hurt? The Meaning of Christian Suffering* (P&R Publishing, 1998), 38, 40. Emphasis original.

6   David Gibson, *Living Life Backward: How Ecclesiastes Teaches Us to Live in Light of the End* (Crossway, 2017), 57–58.

Chapter 6: The Wait of Glory

1   If you are experiencing thoughts of suicide, David Powlison's *I Just Want to Die: Replacing Suicidal Thoughts with Hope* (New Growth Press, 2010) may be a helpful resource.

2   "Right Now Counts Forever" was the title of R.C. Sproul's column in *Tabletalk* magazine.

3   Frederick William Danker, ed., *A Greek-English Lexicon of the New Testament and Other Early Christian Literature*, 3rd ed. (University of Chicago Press, 2000), Logos, under "katergázomai."

4   David Gibson, *Living Life Backward: How Ecclesiastes Teaches Us to Live in Light of the End* (Crossway, 2017), 56.

5   Commentary on 1 Peter 1:7, in Matthew Henry, *Commentary on the Whole Bible*. Available online at https://www.ccel.org/h /henry/mhc2/.

6   Notes on "The Book of Habakkuk," in *Reformation Study Bible*, ed. R.C. Sproul (Reformation Trust Publishing, 2015).

7   Joni Eareckson Tada, *A Place of Healing: Wrestling with the Mysteries of Suffering, Pain, and God's Sovereignty* (David C Cook, 2010), 104.

8   Tada, 107–8.

9   See Terrence Malick, dir., *A Hidden Life* (Fox Searchlight Pictures, 2019).

10   Tada, *A Place of Healing*, 100.

Chapter 7: Weeping in Hurt

1   Mark Vroegop, *Dark Clouds, Deep Mercy: Discovering the Grace of Lament* (Crossway, 2019), 28.

2   Zack Eswine, *Recovering Eden: The Gospel According to Ecclesiastes* (P&R Publishing, 2014), 28–29, 83–84.

3   Kelly M. Kapic, *Embodied Hope: A Theological Meditation on Pain and Suffering* (IVP Academic, 2017), 31.

4   Christopher Ash, *Job: The Wisdom of the Cross*, Preaching the Word (Crossway, 2014), 74, 128.

Conclusion

1   John Bunyan, *Pilgrim's Progress*, 1678; available online at https:// www.monergism.com/pilgrims-progress-ebook-0.

Appendix: How to Help Those Who Face Comprehensive and Chronic Suffering

1   Kelly M. Kapic, *Embodied Hope: A Theological Meditation on Pain and Suffering* (IVP Academic, 2017), 153–54.

2   Benjamin B. Warfield, *The Emotional Life of Our Lord*, in *The Person and Work of Christ*, ed. John J. Hughes (P&R Publishing, 2023), 116.

3   Warfield, 123.

4   Warfield, 124, quoting John Calvin.

5   Warfield, 129.

ALSO FROM P&R PUBLISHING

Whether you're a parent, spouse, child, or friend, when your loved one's life is wracked by illness and pain, your life changes too. Nate Brooks's *Disrupted Journey* is an honest, deeply personal book that helps caregivers and companions of hurting people to process their own upended lives, relationships, and spiritual walk—while keeping their gaze on the comfort and hope offered by Scripture.

"You are not alone in this journey. Here is someone in solidarity who 'gets it,' who offers hard-earned wisdom, and who is willing to be vulnerable so he might help others. May this book strengthen many, and may it equip well-meaning ministers and friends who want to better understand the realities of family life for those with chronic pain."
—**Kelly M. Kapic**, Author, *Embodied Hope: A Theological Meditation on Pain and Suffering*

From **P&R** *and the* **BIBLICAL COUNSELING COALITION**

In the 31-Day Devotionals for Life series, biblical counselors and Bible teachers guide you through Scripture passages that speak to specific situations or struggles, helping you to apply God's Word to your life in practical ways day after day.

Did you find this book helpful?
Consider leaving a review online.
The author appreciates your feedback!

Or write to P&R at editorial@prpbooks.com
with your comments. We'd love to hear from you.